Prison Management, Prison Workers, and Prison Theory

Prison Management, Prison Workers, and Prison Theory

Alienation and Power

Stephen C. McGuinn

LEXINGTON BOOKS
Lanham • Boulder • New York • London

Published by Lexington Books
An imprint of The Rowman & Littlefield Publishing Group, Inc.
4501 Forbes Boulevard, Suite 200, Lanham, Maryland 20706
www.rowman.com

Unit A, Whitacre Mews, 26–34 Stannary Street, London SE11 4AB

British Library Cataloguing in Publication Information Available

Library of Congress Cataloging-in-Publication Data

McGuinn, Stephen C., 1979–
Prison management, prison workers, and prison theory / Stephen C. McGuinn.
  pages cm
Includes bibliographical references and index.
ISBN 978-0-7391-9433-1 (cloth : alk. paper)—ISBN 978-0-7391-9434-8 (electronic)
1. Prison administration—United States. 2. Corrections—United States.
3. Imprisonment—United States. I. Title.
HV9469.M355 2015
365.068—dc2   2014036856

∞™ The paper used in this publication meets the minimum requirements of American National Standard for Information Sciences—Permanence of Paper for Printed Library Materials, ANSI/NISO Z39.48-1992.

Printed in the United States of America

Contents

Acknowledgments

This project was possible because of great external support. I am greatly indebted to my family. Thank you, Katie Grace. I love you. You are relentlessly warm. Thanks to you as well, Gia. You are joy. And to you Willoughby; you bring such happiness. I would also like to thank a few exceptional mentors. To Charles Wellford: thank you for your sharp eye, direct critique, and persistent support. Your guidance and advice were truly beneficial. Your knowledge and reach extend far beyond normal borders. To Ray Paternoster: I could not thank you enough for your patience, quick and keen insight, and spectacular theoretical vision. You are the humble master of a large land and I am truly appreciative of your support and wisdom. To David Maimon: I thank you for your kind and inexorable mentorship. I am incredibly grateful.

.

Chapter 1

Introduction

Prisons should be instruments of justice. Their collective effect should be to promote and not to undermine, society's aspirations for a fair distribution of rights, resources, and opportunities.

—National Research Council (2014, 323)

Imprisonment is a fierce instrument of the state. The US criminal justice system relies heavily on this instrument. Prisons in the United States incarcerate over 1.5 million men and women (Carson and Golinelli 2013). Jails house an additional 726,000 (Minton 2012). But this is a modern reliance. Six times as many men and women are incarcerated today as compared to the early 1970s (Pettit and Western 2004; National Research Council 2014). Close to 1% of the US adult population is currently imprisoned (Pew Center on the States 2008). With 4.2 million on probation and over 800,000 on parole, recent estimates conclude that about 3% of American adults are under correctional supervision (Pew Center on the States 2009). Although a fraction of the size of state facilities, federal prisons and jails still detain about 215,000 people (US Department of Justice 2014). Raw numbers only tell part of the story. The United States disproportionately incarcerates people of color and the poor (National Research Council 2014). Among high school dropouts, more black males are in prison than in the workforce (National Research Council 2014). The disparity in incarceration practices has led some scholars to call US criminal justice policy "hyper incarceration" (Wacquant 2010). Imprisonment is a tremendous state power. But it is only reasonable if it is legitimate, and it is only legitimate if the public perceives it to be fairly and consistently applied. In particular, those most impacted by the modern era of mass incarceration need to perceive fairness in the system, otherwise the goals of punishment, that is, the goals of prison, are likely ineffective.

The prison buildup over the past 40 years far exceeded its utility, this much is clear (National Research Council 2014). Yet, if decarceration policies spread across the United States, as the National Research Council appropriately advises, then prisoner composition will also shift. Correctional managers, sentencing experts, and the public in general should anticipate the potential for this shift. The current era is an appropriate occasion to directly address the rationale for the prison and the essential requirements of the prison institution. Diverting select populations *away* from prison subtly defines prison. I agree that the reduction in current imprisonment rates is an unequivocal good. But there are consequences to such action. If decarceration is implemented properly, then the resultant prisoner population will be those who are truly unfit for civil liberty and who truly threaten public order. In this world, prisons themselves are logical places of confinement and reflect and endorse reasonable intention. Although actual decarceration may prove to be a complicated and slow process, modern theoretical and philosophical development of prison intention does not need to be. Clear declarations of prison intention will help to lead the movement toward effective and selective incarceration strategies.

Primarily, this book is about managing prisons within a rational and clear statement of intention. Prisoners and public perceptions are only indirectly addressed in this book. Instead, I argue that prison workers are the essential actors of importance within the prison. I further reason that prison administrators define the culture and the morality of prison through these prison workers. The relationship between prison workers and prison managers is central to effective prison management. Effective managers prioritize prison workers in order to meet external societal demands of imprisonment and internal demands of daily operation. Safe, humane, and progressive prisons develop from strong staff relationships—irrespective of prisoner composition. Prison administrators need to legitimize the institution for prison staff *and* reduce the naturally alienating conditions of prison work. This position contends that alienation is a key phenomenon of interest in prison work. This position also contends that prison managers need to ensure that they adopt constructive power strategies to meet institutional goals.

Although the nature of effective prison management encourages alienating practices, the effects of such practices may be minimized with moderate adjustments (without compromising central management strategies). Relationships are essential to prison work (Liebling 2004)—but the relationship between staff and prisoners is not the only relationship. Prison staff interact and depend on supervisors and on coworkers. Behavioral, social, and individual complications that arise through prison work are arguably a result of alienation engendered through supervisors and coworkers. I argue that the key variables captured by alienation measures will reduce the harm that management strategies have on staff without compromising safety or security.

Prison clearly impacts prisoners *and* prison workers. And a sizeable work force is required to maintain state and federal prisons. The Bureau of Prisons employs over 38,000 men and women to supervise the prisoner populations across 117 institutions (Samuels 2014). And the culture that prison administrators promote matters. The prison institution is regulated, supervised, and run by correctional staff and administrators. Prisoners can generate severe complications for management, but management sets protocol and is responsible (and held accountable) for the safety, security, and effectiveness of the institution. In strict security settings, I propose that meaning is largely derived through the hierarchy and through coworkers. Reducing alienation among prison staff—by targeting these key relationships—will help to ensure that the priorities of prison management (and the intention of prison in general) can be effectively met.

In addition, prisons are able to employ a variety of power strategies to meet their needs of confinement. But the *ability* to employ power does not necessarily imply the *right* to employ power. Setting aside the goals of punishment, prisons are designed to forcibly confine men and women and to physically remove them from civil society and place them in cells. Historical perspectives on the reasoning for this process vary but the central component of forced confinement is a severe and eerie symbol of power. Those who normalize prison culture (and normalize prison itself) tend to forget this reality. We should be wary of the awesome power of imprisonment and we should mete out its wrath to as few people as possible. Although I do believe that the state needs to wield such power, it should be used with impressive moderation. The state should be acutely aware of the legitimacy of the prison institution. This does not speak merely to the public's perception. Within the facility itself, increased institutional legitimacy—or the general belief that the prison has a right to punish and punishes fairly within that right—results in increased formal rule adherence and reduces informal and inconsistent management deployment.

Prison management is complex. In the next few pages, I briefly detail important themes that appear throughout the book. This introduction serves to help amplify the nuanced and often contradictory nature of prison management. These truncated discussions also illustrate a few unfortunate and occasionally baseless (but popular) assumptions about the prison environment. This chapter also begins a more abstract discussion about the purpose and the place of prison in modern civil society. In subsequent chapters, I further theoretical and philosophical positions on the rationale and intention of forced confinement.

THE CONTEXT OF PRISON MANAGEMENT

The modern age of prison management largely focuses on security through order maintenance. Ineffective policies reflective of the New Penology doctrine (DiIulio 1991b; Marquart and Roebuck 1985)—coupled with rising crime and the perceived futile role of rehabilitation—transformed prison management. Adopting security as its strict focus in the 1980s, prison management philosophy sought to enhance professionalism and procedure (see Lombardo 1989). Riots and prison violence were considered consequences of inept and even careless oversight (Useem and Kimball 1989; see also Useem and Piehl 2006; Useem and Goldstone 2002)—not the inevitable outcomes of the prison itself. This new evolution lauded strong central authorities and adherence to formal rule enforcement. Security in prison is critical and the physical protection of prison workers and of prisoners cannot be compromised for other ends. But these perspectives are not without consequences.

In practice, modern prison management generates a considerable degree of nuance, complexity, and ambiguity. Accountability revolves around adherence to official decree (Lombardo 1989). Evading blame for security lapses is unofficially encouraged and reduces commitment to peers or fellow workers. The subsequent emotional separation of the prison worker from his peers, from his supervisors, and from prisoners is therefore likely inevitable (see Lombardo 1989). This context engenders an environment of individual survival that revolves around the self and not around the collective. Consequently, power strategies employed on the unit are likely to differ from power adoptions officially sanctioned. Indeed, selective rule enforcement may be necessary to avoid reprimands from a supervisor who would assume incompetence when faced with a high volume of written infractions. Of course, a single worker is unlikely to eliminate infractions by a population predisposed to rule violation. But a single worker can reduce evidence of infractions. There is incentive, therefore, to manage one's unit independent of the whole, especially if doing so ensures low visibility. Thus, it is likely that the modern age of prison management implicitly requires alienated workers and simultaneously (and perhaps unintentionally) promotes informal power adoptions.

MEANING, INNOVATION, AND CRIMINAL JUSTICE THEORY DEVELOPMENT

Prison workers do not work in a theoretical environment. Even though the keeper philosophy condemns acts of violence within the institutional setting because victimization would be an added punishment for detained men and women, correctional officers are human actors, seasoned by a complex and often difficult and needy population. It is perhaps undeniable that inside prison walls there are those who frequently strive to employ violence and manipulation to achieve desired ends. While it may be convenient to casually demand superior levels of care in our prisons, we generally ask others to provide this care and we may overlook the complexity of providing appropriate care to those whose freedoms must be restricted. Our lack of interest only helps to exacerbate this internally isolating condition: "[f]eeling that they are abused by inmates, unappreciated by superiors, unsupported by colleagues, guards tend to think they are fighting a lost cause" (Poole and Regoli 1981, 258). This context helps to engender meaninglessness in the work.

In addition, the wave of returning prisoners is significant. Although the Bureau of Prisons specifically promotes innovation in effective prisoner programming, recidivism rates (see Durose, Cooper, and Snyder 2014) suggest inadequacies in prison programming and/or in released offenders. Of course, selection effects make it difficult to assess the effects of the prison environment on ex-prisoners (Useem and Piehl 2008; but see MacKenzie, Bierie, and Mitchell 2007). But something is failing and it is not always easy to identify the cause. It is not unrealistic to propose that the revolving door of prison diminishes the sense of meaning in prisoner supervision. From this localized perspective, the prison experience does not appear to deter nor does programming appear to rehabilitate. But unless prison workers perceive their work to be meaningful—and for their investment of time and effort to be worthwhile—then implementation of effective programming in prisons is unlikely. This is unfortunate because rehabilitation can work (MacKenzie 2006). Taken to its logical extreme, alienation of prison workers may directly hamper effective innovation implementation, which may hinder adequate drops in prison populations in the coming years.

It is possible that the future success of prisons may be based on their ability to "fix" offenders. With recidivism rates as high as they are—with 4 in 10 returning to state prisons within three years (Pew Center on the States 2011)—it is not clear that the public will not begin to demand more from the price of institutionalization. Research may identify effective programming for current offenders. But if prisons are not held accountable for successful implementation, then there is no incentive to implement those programs and to ensure that implementation is successful. If most who go in eventually get out, then it is in our interest to ensure that one main goal of prison management is the reduction in recidivism. This book suggests that empowerment, transparency, and skill provision dramatically improve institutional commitment and efficacy in prisoner management. These improvements may make prison environments fertile grounds for program innovation. In addition, empowerment may improve humane treatment of prisoners, which may increase the public's opinion of the prison worker (subsequently improving the meaning in the work). I propose that injecting meaning, purpose, and communal responsibility into prison work may be possible without compromising safety. Ultimately, sincere efforts should be made to minimize the negative effects of alienation on prison workers.

Criminal justice theory is sparse. But as Kraska (2006, 171) writes: "understanding the why of criminal justice behavior is crucial for the effective development and implementation of policy and reforms." I propose that modern prisons informally and formally promote alienation practices—due in large part to a strict focus on order maintenance and security—and that these practices reduce the effectiveness of prison management and dehumanize prison workers. Unlike criminological theories that propose reasons for crime commission, this criminal justice theory proposes an inevitable (and, to a degree, necessary) impact of modern coercive institutions on prison workers and on prisoners. This perspective is advantageous because management strategies and prisoner programming will not succeed without prison worker acceptance (see Rogers 2003). That which empowers workers and improves their perceptions of prisoner management will also facilitate implementation of innovation. Prison should work for the prisoner *and* for the prison worker. Increasing the perception that he is of value and contributes substantially to the success of the prison likely will improve the possibility that advanced programming can be introduced not as an undue "advantage" to the prisoner but rather as a tool to further the prison worker's own personal success, his unit's success, and his institution's success at actually making the world less dangerous.

PRISON WORKERS IN PRISON

Prisons are uniform neither in management practices (DiIulio 1987) nor in security classification. Nor do I believe researchers can assume inherent flaws and immorality in their mere use and existence (see Zimbardo, Maslach, and Haney 2000). Prisons require state actors to voluntarily manage populations that courts deem unfit for unrestrained societal interaction. I believe that it would be presumptuous to assume that the prison officer marks or labels the newly incarcerated independent of, and without assistance from, general social consensus. Prison sentencing is a social statement about the fitness of the individual to conduct himself properly—generally due to prior conduct but arguably with the implicit assumption that it is predictive of future conduct. It would not be surprising, from this genesis (birthed in codified law), if the prison officer adopted or furthered his opinion of prisoners through daily experience and constant interaction. Indeed, I admit that the prison worker's perspective could advance to an inappropriate and indefensible perspective. But I propose that this judgment begins in the social conscience, reinforced by our demand for prisons, reinforced by our crime rates, reinforced by general consensus, and ever present upon institutional admission:

> The interpretative scheme of the total institution automatically begins to operate as soon as the inmate enters, the staff having the notion that entrance is *prima facie* evidence that one must be the kind of person the institution was set up to handle. . . . A man in prison must be a lawbreaker. . . . (Goffman 1961, 84)

But it is reasonable for the prison worker to assume that those entering prison as inmates are in fact lawbreakers. It is reasonable in that it reflects belief in the rule of law, in the fairness and objectivity of the state, and of due process. There is nothing inherent in this assumption alone—one that is based on the foundation that prisons do exist and that men and women are held in them against their will—that is problematic. The problem arises when the status gained by admission to a facility earns particular responses regardless of the individual's present behavior but based upon the status. But this behavior is rejected by the modern keeper philosophy. In contemporary prison settings, the keeper philosophy views prison as punishment enough (DiIulio 1987; Jurik and Musheno 1986). Goffman's (1961) assumption appears to be that institutional staff act on inappropriate bias. The occurrence of such behavior in modern prisons, I propose, would be due to ineffective prison management rather than official prison management philosophy. It is more likely that modern prison management has increased the likelihood that the prison worker does not even actively consider the prisoner.

It is also plausible that actual bias arrives from outside assumptions about the insides of prisons. I believe that it is quite possible that the sheer horror of prolonged and confined isolation in cages is magnified by those who have rare opportunity to visit or whose understanding of the prison environment has been garnered through social consumption and not through prison itself. This is not to excuse or condone the practice of institutionalization. But it is to challenge the assumption that increased exposure to such an environment automatically engenders negative mental and physical health outcomes. The implicit assumption in prison literature—especially in correctional officer literature—is that prison work must be dangerous, awful, stressful, and detrimental to a series of health, social, and mental health outcomes. The Stanford Prison Experiment was infamous for promoting the extreme of this perspective, one that Zimbardo still lauds: "the value of the Stanford Prison Experiment (SPE) resides in demonstrating the evil that good people can be readily induced into doing to other good people within the context of socially approved roles, rules, and norms, a legitimizing ideology, and institutional support that transcends individual agency" (Zimbardo, Maslach, and Haney 2000, 1). The intended context here is the prison, which, by its very nature, is considered to be inhumane and suggests that those who operate it, likewise, are inhumane. This claim, of course, flows from a simulated prison experiment that lasted six days. Perhaps an opposing contention would suggest that this could be an artifact flowing out of the specifics of the arranged conditions.

Indeed, the conclusions from the SPE were not drawn from actual prison observations. Students became guards or prisoners without prior prison experience. Their assumption of prison could only be based on their understanding of prison, which was not derived from actual experience. Equally, to an unseasoned officer, it is quite plausible that external social definitions of prisons—largely gained through collective assumptions and furthered, for example, by media portrayal—will influence and inform not only his understanding of prison but also his attitude toward prisoners and prison work. It could be contended that the results of the SPE and the very experiment itself are largely an artifact, induced by a false context of inexperienced participants. Barring exposure to actual prison environments, these participants could either be selecting into the experiment because they are more likely to be aggressive and antisocial individuals (see Carnahan and McFarland 2007) or they could be adopting authoritarian positions during the experiment because their only comprehension of prison officers and prison management arrives via secondhand, even tainted, commercial and dramatized sources. Both possibilities undermine the value of the results relative to the authentic nature of confinement. Perhaps, most importantly though, we have real prisons in the United States—why analyze simulations? In all fairness, of course, it is important to note that it is possible that Zimbardo's overall claim has less to do with actual prisons and more to do with the ease with which good people can be coerced into terrible behaviors. But it is less clear that general audiences distinguish between this nuanced inference and the misplaced assumption about inevitable prison effects. Prison workers do not have the luxury of working outside of public perception. And unfavorable public perception will diminish the meaning in prison work.

Of course, this discussion is not intended to suggest that prisons are therefore humane and that prison workers do not judge prisoners and do not act inappropriately. But it is a remarkable fact that older and more senior correctional officers—with lengthier exposure to these "horrible" prison environments—hold much more favorable views toward prisoners and toward treatment (Farkas 1999; Toch and Klofas 1982; Schaufeli and Peeters 2000; Paboojian and Teske 1997). It is unimportant whether older officers have merely survived attrition due to burnout, cynicism, and other detrimental outcomes. Either the prison environment does not impact certain types of people or the prison environment improves attitudes over time. Indeed, careful selection of prison workers would undermine the "inevitable" damage. Perhaps, randomly assigning people to prison work, by *definition*, would be inappropriate and harmful.

INEVITABLE PRISON ENVIRONMENTS?

Prisons house those who, by legal definitions, are not "good." It is likely that certain populations require confinement (this cannot be understated). If prisons are necessary for select populations (e.g., excessively violent men and women), then it is difficult to equate appropriate social behavior in greater society to appropriate management in confined society. This difficulty does not preclude humane treatment while in facility but *different* treatment. This is to emphasize that prisons might be necessary, given the current populations of offenders. I do not make this point to condone the incarceration of 1% of the US adult population. The challenge may not be to abolish prisons but to "right-size" them (Useem and Piehl 2008).

The assumption that prison institutions automatically create an environment that is contrary to humanity and to rehabilitation either arises from an assumption that collections of monstrous inmates will automatically overrun and manage the prison with or without official support or that something about the actual structure of confinement—literally caging men and women in cells—is so foreign to the human skin that it breeds torture, corruption, and abuse (Zimbardo, Maslach, and Haney 2000). Arguably, these two positions are not entirely incompatible. But the first instance would have to prove that prison violence and mayhem are inevitable outcomes, irrespective of management strategies. And the second instance would again need to prove that prolonged exposure to prison environments—both by inmates and by correctional officers—inevitably leads to misuse of power, abuse, and (in Zimbardo's lexicon) "evil." It is probable that neither of these perspectives reflects the authentic nature of the prison environment and that both are mild to severe caricatures of the actual prison experience as evidenced by those who volunteer to work there and those who involuntarily are recruited as residents. More likely, in fact, is the development of a more subtle perspective:

> Given the inmates of whom they have charge, and the processing that must be done to them, the staff tend to evolve what may be thought of as a theory of human nature. As an implicit part of institutional perspective, this theory rationalizes activity, provides a subtle means of maintaining social distance from inmates and a stereotypes view of them, and justifies the treatment accorded to them. (Goffman 1961, 87)

As opposed to the crude and dehumanizing image illustrated by Zimbardo and his colleagues, Goffman (1961) paints a more nuanced and plausible scenario in which institutional officers are biased and judgmental but not necessarily *evil*. This perspective, appropriately, permits the outside social environment to help reinforce the institutional worker's opinion of the prisoner. It may not merely be the nature of the institution that is driving the personality and responses of the prison officer; it may also be the influence of general social opinion and the critical awareness that institutions hold specific types of people—and prisons hold lawbreakers. After all, the state sends men and women to prison. Rather than assume that prisons themselves necessarily produce harmful outcomes, it is preferable to demonstrate that management strategies generate a type of environment that may be beneficial to security but less beneficial to meaningful prison work. If we accept the fact that we need prisons, we must then seek to adopt prisons that best serve those who volunteer to oversee them and best detain those who involuntarily reside within them. This point is central.

BOOK OUTLINE

Chapter 2 provides an overview of prison management in the United States. Particular attention is paid to current and past management perspectives. The historical and current use of prison in the United States is discussed in this chapter. In addition, I advance the need for a clear understanding of the purpose of prison within an evolving criminal justice system. Chapter 3 briefly details the analytical strategy employed in this book (and is intended for the more technical readers). Chapter 4 illustrates the importance of power in prison environments and evaluates power strategies adopted by federal prison workers and the effect that power adoptions have on perceived efficacy of prisoner management. Chapter 5 demonstrates the integral role of alienation in coercive environments and shows (1) how prison worker alienation diminishes effective prisoner management and (2) how alienation dehumanizes prison workers. Chapter 6 provides a foundation for a criminal justice theory of prisons. Chapter 7 concludes the book, summarizes key findings, and suggests important directions for future inquiry.

Chapter 2

Prison Management

THE NEW PENOLOGY

In 1958, Gresham Sykes contended that prison subcultures unavoidably form: the inevitable nature of incarceration and the close proximity of inmates would engender oppositional collectives. Sykes even suggested that attempts to limit subculture generation could be counter to effective safety management since these bodies would actively resist external (or foreign) intervention and sanction. This perspective fed the development of the *New Penology* (DiIulio 1991b), a philosophy that promoted inmate self-policing. Several systems adopted variations on this practice and assumed the validity of this "inescapable" reality. As an extreme example, Texas prison officials largely passed supervision duties onto the prisoners. Officers selected inmates to oversee housing units and to notify authorities of rule violations. Labeled "building tenders" and "turnkeys," these prisoners would actually carry gate keys and supervise fellow prisoners (Marquart and Roebuck 1985). These specific tactics directly reflected the essential premise of the *New Penology*: "prisons must be governed by prisoners themselves" (DiIulio 1991b, 72). Correctional officers in Texas largely outsourced the direct management of housing populations. This strategy failed. Appeals courts eventually overturned self-governing inmate practices as cruel and unusual punishment (Marquart and Roebuck 1985). Prisoners did not protect their "constituents" from excessive and systematic abuse and harm (Marquart and Roebuck 1985). One potential lesson from this dangerous adoption: prison workers (and only prison workers) should directly manage and discipline prisoners.

Inmate subcultures may evolve into aggressive and resistant bodies. But democratic governance is not a plausible course of action for successful control and oversight of institutional charges. I do not suggest that choice is categorically unreasonable within the prison setting. Choices of vocational training, of academic pursuits, or of artistic endeavors are reasonable and do not require security compromises. But prisoner choice in institutional management and in protocol is inappropriate. Prisoners, by definition, have proven their inability to abide by the collective will. Although transformation and assimilation are likely necessary for effective reentry, it seems presumptuous and ill-informed to place such responsibility on a collective body rather than to place responsibility on the individual actors who can and will desist from criminal behavior. Diversity exists within the prison population and prisoners do not recidivate at the same rate (Petersilia 2003) or respond favorably to the same treatment modules (MacKenzie 2006). I agree that prison management should *correct*—it should believe in rehabilitating the prisoner to the extent that is possible. But this cannot come at the cost of security and this cannot assume that the prison population is homogeneous. If implemented authentically, prisoner self-governance makes an assumption of homogeneity, assumes the benevolence of a prisoner hierarchy of leadership, presumes prisoner comprehension of effective treatment, and downplays the dangerousness of factions. Safety measures within prisons cannot overlook the weakest prisoners—or bend to the demands of the majority at even slight cost to a minority population. Democratic or majority rule, by definition, is improper within prison institutions.

The *New Penology* was a dangerous and failed experiment in prison management. Unchallenged premises in this time suggested that prison management itself may be impossible. But in the late 1980s and early 1990s, research emerged that promoted effective management strategies (DiIulio 1987) and riot prevention (Useem and Kimball 1989; see also Useem and Goldstone 2002; Useem and Piehl 2006) through increased focus in security and command structure. Although the crime rate was soaring and fears and rumors about new "super-predators" were circulating (DiIulio 1995), research surfaced that suggested safe prisons could exist—even in this climate. Indeed, the same proponent of the super-predator also promoted what would become the model of prison management.

SECURITY FIRST

DiIulio (1987; 1991b) contended that enhanced levels of security (order), amenity, and service effectively arrive through "politically astute leadership, an organizational culture built around 'security-first' goals, and a paramilitary organizational structure" (DiIulio 1991b, 82). In essence, prisons can be managed and prisons can be safe. At the same time, prison riot analysis suggested that 1970s prison violence was avoidable (Useem and Kimball

1989). Riots erupted because management failed to follow protocol and failed to utilize tools and measures within its arsenal that would have protected officers and inmates from lethal violence. This research suggested that it was not management per se but inattentive and even careless management that led to those horrific and lethal outcomes (Useem and Kimball 1989; see also Useem and Piehl 2006; Useem and Goldstone 2002). Regardless of prisoner composition, this literature also suggested that safe prisons were possible. By taking appropriate steps, prison administrators could actually control and successfully supervise prisoner populations.

There is considerable benefit to the security-first model. Security-first models empower prison workers and demonstrate administrative solidarity with prison staff. But these models are not germane only to security. When Rhode Island adopted a security-first platform, for example, it did not abandon rehabilitation (Carroll 1998). The new mission of corrections in Rhode Island targeted "the protection of society through the provision of safe, secure, and humane control of offenders" (Carroll 1998, 314). The official adoption of a rational and security-first mission led to internal stability (Carroll 1998) and arguably made Rhode Island corrections publicly legitimate. But even though rehabilitation faded from view as the first priority of corrections, it did not disappear from inside prisons. In fact, programming in Rhode Island improved in quality and in breadth after rehabilitation lost its priority status (Carroll 1998). This is an important lesson. I reason that prioritizing security and safety acknowledges the difficulty of prison work and recognizes the prior deviance of the prisoner population. From this platform, rehabilitation is more tenable since it becomes a tool for population management and not an undue benefit (I discuss this in depth in subsequent sections). I further infer that prison administrators in the United States are wise to officially (and publicly) endorse security first models. These models may be necessary for public mollification, for safe prisons, *and* for rehabilitation. It is not surprising that safety is the first goal of the Bureau of Prisons (USDOJ 2010). But this does not imply that BOP has abandoned rehabilitation.

The rehabilitation effort of the first part of the twentieth century might have been short on substance in many states (Carroll 1998). And due to the current political climate at the beginning of the twenty-first century (and the general perception of prisoners), effective rehabilitation may require a degree of subtle cleverness in order to win over prison staff and the public (Kaplan 2014). More to the point, rehabilitation may be inappropriate and ineffective as an official and internal priority. If prison workers perceive that their jobs and their lives are the priority of prison managers then flexibility in prisoner programming may increase without substantial resistance. Without this clear assurance, prison systems may suffer as a result. New York City's Department of Corrections, for example, is plagued by the disconnect between prison workers and the prison hierarchy (see Schwirtz 2014). These disconnects have dangerous consequences. Prisons house dangerous and violent individuals. Prison workers understand this. But security-first measures protect and empower prison workers and reinforce their integral role in the successful administration of justice in the United States. A system that first respects the worker can then reform the captive. It is not my intention to undermine or discount the importance of rehabilitation. The delivery, however, of effective treatment programming may require finesse and administrative loyalty.

DISCRETION AND ORDER IN PRISON

Contemporary prison management philosophies illustrate formal acknowledgment that detainment is punishment enough and that no inmate should suffer from assault, rape, or murder (DiIulio 1987; Jurik and Musheno 1986; Bureau of Prisons 2011). Prisons operate as key limiters on human freedom, and the legitimacy of corrections is compromised without this condition. But uniform procedures may not be sufficient (or practical) for effective prisoner management. Since fairness and consistency in oversight are inherent in legitimacy, additional factors complicate legitimate management in practice. The prison administration may codify illegal behaviors and may define contraband. But universal rule enforcement may be counterproductive. In fact, effective control measures may actually violate institutional code *and* simultaneously reduce friction with supervisors and with charges:

> A guard cannot rely on the direct application of force to achieve compliance for he is one man against hundreds; and if he continually calls for additional help he becomes a major problem for the shorthanded prison administration . . . the guard, then, is under pressure to achieve a smoothly running cellblock not with the stick but with the carrot, but here again his stock of rewards is limited. One of the best "offers" he can make is ignoring minor offenses or making sure that he never places himself in a position to discover infractions of the rules. (Sykes 1956, 260)

Strictly speaking, this is an officially unsanctioned *yet* culturally sanctioned role. The complexity necessarily brings a series of conditions that may alter the officer's perception of power and further distance the officer not only from institution ethos but also from the needs of the confined charges. The officer is arguably forced to understand how prison units are to be managed in practice and not by the letter of the rulebook. This additional burden of discretion increases confusion (especially for unseasoned officers) and lends itself to inconsistent treatment across housing units as officers adopt varying strategies of control. But perhaps ironically (at least on the surface), legitimacy requires discretion. Discretion implies the evaluation of context in decision-making. Discretion is vital to fair treatment *because* it distinguishes context and applies judgment:

> Discretion is inevitable where there are rules (and there are too many rules to follow in prison life to make it through the day). Rules and contexts have to be interpreted. . . . Rules are a "resource," rather as relationships can be, in prison. To consider prison life and work as either simply a matter of rule-enforcement, or as unconstrained by rules, is a sociologically impoverished conception. (Liebling 2004, 266)

Legitimate rule enforcement arrives through contextual assessment. Prison workers are asked to evaluate context. Consistent and fair treatment is not simply reflective of systematic rule enforcement. Context creates dissimilar situations and requires judgment—or *expert* power. It is likely that experience and on-site training improve the likelihood of meeting the requirements of this complex environment. Yet, the premise of this discussion is potentially disquieting. Official demands of prison workers cannot contradict unofficial job requirements. To some degree, appropriate behavior must be modeled, condoned, reinforced, and officially reflected in written documents. Either the rulebook must formally endorse prison worker discretion and flexibility (and provide adequate parameters) *or* the prison worker must strictly enforce all the rules, across all populations. Even strict rule enforcement does not require inhumane treatment. Prison workers can be strict and humane. But absolute rule enforcement is probably inappropriate (and unlikely). Context generates situations that warrant departures from codified rule. And autonomy allows prison staff to appear human and reasonable—moved by situational factors: "the legitimate exercise of authority depends on people's experience of the fairness of their treatment, which includes procedures, but also the *manner* of their treatment" (Liebling 2004, 288, italics in original). To some degree, prison workers depend on prisoner agreement. But how does one balance discretion and rule enforcement?

I reason that the fix must be the formal acknowledgement of departures. The burden of discretion is too high without uniformity and clarity. Formal written departures (from codified rules) protect prison workers' discretion, maintain consistency, and enable peer workers to understand contextually acceptable conduct. This approach may be the solution to Liebling's (2004, 267) observation that: "[s]ome resolution between rules in the book and their application in action must therefore be found." Formal departures combine flexibility and accountability and permit the system to be highly rational without appearing inhuman or emotionally compromised.

The allowance improves prison worker ability and, subsequently, improves her connection to her employer. A close bond to the employer (and to the mission of the institution) improves employee morale and improves the consistency with which conflict and problems are addressed (DiIulio 1987).

Admittedly, there are clear prison behaviors that are unconditionally prohibited. The troublesome area arrives with behaviors that are not uniformly (or consistently) rejected by prison staff. I do not seek to abolish discretion. I do seek to justify and formalize discretion. Injecting clarity and accountability in the form of written documentation does not undermine the power or utility of discretion. Discretion is integral to prison management. Individual discretion permits officers to solve individual—and perhaps even unique—problems that arise throughout the course of their tour. Although strict order maintenance may protect prisoners from physical harm (DiIulio 1987), strong administrative authorities that depend solely on strict rule enforcement strategies may not be sufficient. Order maintenance benefits from malleability. But I do not advocate for informality. Urbane inmate populations are unlikely. Nuanced approaches to supervision, which rely on informalities, are likely to increase the probability of abuse. Formal departure keeps prison staff faithful to institution mission, reduces the likelihood of informal relationships between prisoners and prison staff, and improves worker solidarity.

This proposition of "amended" governance highlights the value of formality. Formality improves order and order impacts safety. In prison, safety involves both staff and prisoner safety. The breakdown of administrative control, or mismanagement largely due to the miscommunication or lack of mission clarity, arguably led to a series of riots in the 1970s and 1980s in which both officers and inmates fell victim to violence (Useem and Kimball 1989; see also Useem and Goldstone 2002; Useem and Piehl 2006). Poor administrative care and misguided trust in inmate self-government appear to lead to ineffective protection of the most needy and vulnerable of inmate populations (see Useem and Kimball 1989; Marquart and Roebuck 1985; DiIulio 1991b; see also Useem and Piehl 2006). Strong central organization, without ceding valuable discretion away from the correctional officer, allows for transparency in rule enforcement. This arrangement is favorable from an order maintenance and safety perspective. But these ideas are not new. Two and one-half centuries ago, Beccaria (1995 [1764], 17) insisted that "the more people understand the sacred code of the laws . . . the fewer will be the crimes." Knowing the rules and knowing that those rules will be enforced fairly and appropriately may impact behaviors in and out of prisons. This is rational oversight. This applies to prison workers as well as to prisoners. Reasons for professional conduct, or reasons for allowed departures, should be easily justified if they are indeed reasonable.

Adopting a complex model for discretion requires strong central leadership. Long-tenured directors with proactive and intimate knowledge of their facilities who are extremely loyal breed high morale among their staff (DiIulio 1987, 242). Useem and Piehl (2006, 107) observe that "a substantial body of evidence, based on in-depth case studies, shows that level of order depends crucially upon the quality of political and correctional leadership." Management practices (and perceptions thereof) may directly impact officer attitude toward the institution, which may then directly impact the ability of a prison to run safely and humanely. In addition, a sense of fairness may also impact prisoner and prison worker morale. The manner in which problems and grievances are tackled by supervising bodies (for both inmates and officers), as well as the predictability of that body's support, should affect morale. It is unsurprising that distant and unsympathetic oversight may erode the effectiveness of management and strict staff rule adherence—thereby opening the door for an individualized system where independent operators are merely concerned with avoiding blame (see Lombardo 1989). Prisons are complex environments. Even security-first goals are nuanced endeavors.

THE DETACHED KEEPER

In his notable confrontation with sociological dogma, DiIulio (1987) contends that proper prison administration is sufficient and necessary for effective order maintenance. Although greatly outnumbered in the facility, effective prison managers may successfully provide quality oversight that reduces disorder, improves treatment facilitation, and may even produce less dire recidivism rates (see DiIulio 1987, 40–48). DiIulio's (1987) model imposes rationality and consistency into management style. Managers need not rely on inmate approval or buy-in per se to achieve success. Instead, the appropriate injection of order, amenity, and service ensure humane imprisonment (DiIulio 1987, 11–12). Prisoners are not denied access to treatment services; they are not denied reasonable accommodations; and they are not denied life. Admittedly, this is an argument for a hierarchical, almost dictatorial, approach to prison management. But this is not an argument for brutalization. Indeed, DiIulio (1987, 263) insists that it is a central role of government to maintain safe and humane prisons.

Running safe and humane prisons is no small task. Wardens and line officers must conduct daily business with populations that may horrify the general public (DiIulio 1987, 169). But the purpose of prison is not to augment the prison sentence with cruel treatment. The "keeper" philosophy promotes quite the opposite: "[w]hatever the reason for sending a person to prison, the prisoner is not to suffer pains beyond the deprivation of liberty" (DiIulio 1987, 167; see also Jurik and Musheno 1986). But it is unavoidable that the prison worker must regularly confront antisocial, violent, and manipulative actors. A reasonable model of rational oversight acknowledges inherent—even if latent—institutional conflict. I reason that the preservation of the admirable "keeper" philosophy is challenging, if not impossible. A degree of emotional detachment, therefore, may be advantageous and protect against physical and emotional harm. The burdens of imprisonment should not destroy the prison worker. But it is important to note that the "detached" perspective is not merely beneficial to the prison worker. Since the "keeper" philosophy does not approve of aggravating the prison experience for prisoners, then improving standards of treatment, via rehabilitation, for example, is not in conflict with this perspective. The potentially embedded opposition, between "natural" adversaries, may actually be weakened by the presence of an unemotional guardian.

I am not promoting robotic oversight. I am promoting objectivity. Carroll described the highly effective Rhode Island Department of Corrections as pursuing a "rational, emotionally detached approach to problem-solving" (1998, 313–314). In fact, emotional detachment may encourage impartial care. Contextually derived rule enforcements do improve legitimacy but do not require emotional sacrifice (even though they are individual and personal evaluations). I admit that agreeable prisoners make prison management easier and agreeable prison workers make imprisonment easier. But staff–prisoner relationships are largely evaluated on "instrumental" value and *not* on emotional value (Liebling, Price, and Shefer 2011, 100). Prisoners view prison workers as "gatekeepers" (Liebling et al. 2011, 99) and prison staff rely on "the consent of prisoners in order to 'get through the day'" (Liebling et al. 2011, 132). Although prison staff appear to extol relationships that are "humane and pleasant" (Liebling et al. 2011, 100), this is not emotionally based. I advocate for treatment of prisoners that is fair and consistent and does not inflict physical or emotional pain. I believe this is a necessary (and sufficient) threshold for prison institutions. The keeper philosophy endorses this platform but does not encourage prisoner–staff relationships to exceed their instrumental value. Cordial conduct will improve the instrumental quality of the relationships in prison environments. But emotional engagement biases reason and undermines consistency—a dangerous concession for the legitimacy of the prison institution. Brutality should not and cannot be permitted in prisons, but its natural antithesis is also likely inappropriate.

CUSTODIAL AND TREATMENT ATTITUDES

Positive relationships between prison workers and prisoners do not necessarily generate corrupt staff or clog the effectiveness of prison management. In 1970s Auburn Prison, Lombardo observed: "a positive relationship allows the inmate to approach the officer when a problem is developing, allowing the officer time to defuse it" (1989, 65). During this era, officers at Auburn attempted to keep inmates reasonably supervised and content through advocacy, counseling, and provision of basic services (see Lombardo 1989, 61–64). But by the 1980s, this model began to evaporate, replaced by a more professional and static role:

> Officers [came] to rely on "directives" and directions to determine job tasks and procedures. While it was [in earlier years] relatively common for officers to alter verbal orders to fit individual situations and avoid problems, now the tendency appears to be one of following directives and using directives to justify one's actions to inmates and to superiors. (Lombardo 1989, 69)

Custody orientations largely replaced treatment orientations. Lombardo (1989) details this identity transformation through observations in the 1980s (specifically at Auburn prison in New York state but arguably reflective of a larger trend). Justification of actions to superiors became critical. The command structure became frigid in its hierarchy and individual officers operated within the strict expectations of individual (and perhaps institutional) supervisors. This transition in orientation, with discernible drawbacks, has been presented above as reasonable and necessary in order to promote institutional stability. But it is an unfair generalization to assume that custody and treatment orientations are mutually exclusive. In fact, strict custody-oriented facilities benefit from treatment programming. Rehabilitation helps manage confined populations:

> Most prison and jail administrators view correctional programs from what I have dubbed an *institutional* perspective. They evaluate programs not mainly in terms of what they do to reduce the likelihood of recidivism or otherwise affect inmates' post-release behavior but as institutional management tools. (DiIulio 1991a, 114)

Programming provides "incentives for good inmate behavior" (DiIulio 1991a, 118). Programming keeps prisoners busy, improves communication between staff and charges, improves prisoner assimilation to prison life, and improves officer perception of the utility and importance of their own work (DiIulio 1991a, 114–123; see also Cullen et al. 1989, 1993). Rehabilitation programming (in practice) helps to ensure the safety and security of the prison institution. But rehabilitation itself may also be agreeable to many prison workers. I do not suggest that prisoners' needs should ever trump staff safety in perceived priority (a rash misinterpretation). But most who go into prison will get out (Petersilia 2003)—and most correctional officers subscribe to the idea that "exposing offenders to life-enhancing, skills-imparting programs is likely to help keep at least *some* of them on the straight and narrow" (DiIulio 1991a, 107, italics added). Prison culture is nuanced. Although custody may be the primary goal of prison work, correctional officers call themselves *correctional* officers (rather than guards). This may be due to the perceived professional quality of the label rather than its accuracy, but prior research has found that prison workers are at least privately concerned with treatment (Cullen et al. 1989; Toch and Klofas 1982).

The claim that prison officers are receptive to treatment has, in the past, found empirical support not only among line-staff (Cullen et al. 1989; Toch and Klofas 1982) but also among wardens (Cullen et al. 1993). At first glance, this apparent conflict with the demands of the security-first approach appears problematic. If human-service orientations encourage informal relationships with inmates—even friendliness and personal interactions—and security orientations encourage relationship avoidance and formal interactions with inmates (Hepburn and Knepper 1993) then dual adoption ostensibly calls for the employment of conflicting strategies. But not all agree that security and human-service orientations are actually at odds with one another (see Liebling et al. 2011). Intimate knowledge of prisoners' lives does not necessarily require compromises in security. The focus of the security perspective is to reduce the risk of escape and to reduce internal violence and chaos. Service provision actually helps to meet these outcomes (DiIulio 1987; see also Liebling et al. 2011). And security-first institutions still often promote and employ rehabilitation measures. In addition, reception to treatment does not imply perceived homogeneity of prisoners. Prisoners are not uniformly treatable. It is reasonable for wardens who are supportive of rehabilitative measures to suspect that only one-quarter of prisoners could be—or will be—rehabilitated (Cullen et al. 1993). Wardens probably underestimate the abilities of prisoners but their message is not lost: some individuals are likely to be beyond repair. This is an important point: treatment perspectives may need to coexist with security perspectives—especially if select populations are chronically disposed to antisocial behavior.

In addition, officers tend to believe that coworkers are custody oriented. Individual perception, thereby, may conflict with the public perception of peers (Cullen et al. 1989; see also Toch and Klofas 1982). The resulting culture may be one that is largely custody oriented due to an unwillingness to divulge personal opinion for fear that it may draw ridicule (Cullen et al. 1989). Perceived cultural ideology may mask the authentic composition of correctional attitudes. This is one indicator that prison itself drives culture above and beyond individual differences. But while this culture may fashion the officer in behavior it is not necessarily shaping her attitude. Time on the job may alleviate some discomfort with expressing seemingly oppositional opinions. Older correctional officers may be more willing to share positive perspectives on treatment—perspectives that they may have always had—since they no longer feel controlled by prison ideology (that may or may not even exist). Irrespective of attitude, however, behavior exhibited in facility is what enhances or diminishes treatment efforts. Even if custody orientations dominate prison institutions, behavioral resistance to rehabilitation may not dominate because programming makes population management easier.

Orientation might be more malleable than simply adopting a security *or* a human-service perspective. The prison institution may be able to shape complex ideology (and presumably already does). Whitehead and Lindquist (1989, 83) note: "the organizational whole is greater than the sum of its parts; organizational structure goals and climate are the critical influences on individual employees' orientation." In a sense, the organization can drive the content and the meaning of the orientation. Over time, officers probably become more like one another—regardless of race and gender differences. Research suggesting diverging perceptions due specifically to race and to gender does exist (Britton 1997; see also Jackson and Ammen 1996; Jurik 1985; Jurik and Musheno 1986). But the overall evidence is inconclusive. Close analysis and continued scrutiny of differences are probably warranted. Nevertheless, prison conditions and climate—including organizational factors—arguably play a more important role in shaping prison worker orientation, well-being, and attitude (see Bierie 2012; Whitehead and Lindquist 1989).

We ask a lot from keepers. We demand forfeit of natural liberty for those who have failed to cede even the least of their natural freedom in order to abide the general will that all have the equal right to pursue happiness (Beccaria 1995 [1764]). But in order to monitor those who deviate we ask those who freely cede this natural liberty to the social contract to watch those who have refused. Prisons are necessary—necessary in that they uphold this social contract and promote justice. But it may be remiss to assume that any other employee is asked to do as much as the correctional officer. We ask prison officers to dedicate their entire employment to the welfare of those who have failed to consider the welfare of their neighbor. To add to this, we apparently (at least theoretically) ask that the officer also swallow a great deal of nuance and complexity in the completion of their daily work.

THE HISTORY AND INTENTION OF PRISON IN THE UNITED STATES

Moral Imprisonment?

If prison is used correctly then it conforms to its intention. The intention of prison is historically complex, varied. But it is not unreasonable or illogical to attempt to understand the current purpose—or many purposes—of the prison institution and then to require sentencing to honor that purpose and to act within its potential limitations. This is neither a superficial nor a theoretical proposition. It is insufficient to promote the position that prison meets the goals of punishment without specifying how it accomplishes that feat. Sentenced individuals are entitled to reason—even if that reason is retributive. This minimum requirement of purpose not only is sensible but also allows for adequate institutional evaluation. Thus, prison would retain its prominence (under these conditions) only by clear evidence of effectiveness. Before addressing the utility of prison, I provide a brief historical account of the prison institution in the United States. But first a comment on morality and criminal justice practice.

Understanding imprisonment practices arguably requires an understanding of the prevailing morality and the general perspective toward offenders: "all criminal law is also moral law, again in some regard; every line in the penal code tags some behavior as wrong—either deeply and inherently wrong, or wrong because of its consequences" (Friedman 1993, 125). But collective morality changes across centuries, across continents, and across cultures. And current criminal justice practices reflect current morality: "the history of criminal justice is not only the history of the forms of rewards and punishments; it is also a story about the dominant *morality*, and hence a history of power" (Friedman 1993, 10). This is a salient observation and one that should be applied to current realities. Inadequate adoption or accidental reliance on the prison does not prove or disprove its necessity or its utility. But the past and the present illustrate their (potentially divergent) morality through criminal law and therefore they likely used the prison to achieve divergent outcomes. The larger and more pertinent issue here is that the rationale for excessively high incarceration rates of today should be reconciled with our current morality. Either these rates reflect our moral position and therefore may remain; or they challenge our moral position and therefore must change.

Useem and Piehl (2008, 169) insist that "the prison buildup movement . . . was a pragmatic effort to deal with an escalating crime rate rather than . . . an irrational expression of a disturbed population or an effort to achieve an otherwise extraneous political agenda." This is a valid (and well-supported) claim unless it attempts to evade responsibility for (or downplay) current conditions. I would submit, with some support (see National Research Council 2014), that the imprisonment of close to 1% of American adults (Pew Center on the States 2008) is not "pragmatic"—nor should a movement attached to such an outcome be considered pragmatic. But if we consider current criminal justice practices as reflective of our current collective morality then we must ask ourselves to specifically justify the mass imprisonment of poor black men. We are asked, in this exercise, to acknowledge our collective role in shaping current local and national standards of morality. Fixing prison is much more than fixing what happens within the institution. It demands national public interest and investment. Successful and apparently humane practices employed within prisons in European countries (e.g., Subramanian and Shames 2013) may actually be successful due to historical, cultural, and moral perspectives of forced confinement *in* Europe. But the United States arguably has a unique relationship with prison and a unique relationship with punishment. In this way, the public is integral to prison reform. Prison legitimacy is partly obtained through the perceived fairness and consistency of incarceration. The visceral appeal of imprisonment may be reduced when considered next to the consequences of such a large prison system. Context helps to mitigate the instinctual push for purely retributive models.

Colonial America

The colonial understanding of crime saw little utility in the prison: "the use of the institution in the colonial era was exceptional; few communities depended upon it and even where found, it served only the unusual case" (Rothman 1990, 36). Criminal imprisonment was generally used for those awaiting sentence or awaiting punishment rather than as punishment: "[a] sentence of imprisonment was uncommon, never used alone. Local jails held men caught up in the *process of judgment*. . . . The idea of serving time in prison as a method of correction was the invention of a later generation" (Rothman 1990, 48, italics in original). Communities were small and isolated, residents codependent. These remote and sparsely populated communities could effectively employ shame and expulsion to maintain conformity. It would have been illogical to imprison or unreasonably execute. Instead, colonists attempted to gain submission and conformity through the whip or the fine (Rothman 1990); "[t]he aim was not just to punish, but to teach a lesson, so that the sinful sheep would want to get back to the flock. Punishment tended to be exceedingly public" (Friedman 1993, 37). If these attempts repeatedly failed colonists found recourse in the death penalty; but the death penalty was not the primary tool of punishment (Rothman 1990; Friedman 1993).

To early colonists, sin was crime. Sin largely reflected individual faults rather than community faults (Rothman 1990; Friedman 1993). A collective belief in the spiritual etiology of criminal behavior did not require sophisticated and intermediate punishment strategies. The perceived utility of incarceration may have been minimal: colonists "did not believe that a jail could rehabilitate or intimidate or detain the offender. They placed little faith in the possibility of reform" (Rothman 1990, 53). But rather than rejecting prison, the social conscience of the colonies probably never full embraced the potential utility of imprisonment as punishment: "[t]he penitentiary system was basically a 19th-century invention. Nobody in the colonial period had yet advanced the idea that it was good for the soul, and conducive to reform, to segregate people who committed crimes, and keep them behind bars" (Friedman 1993, 48). The colonists' insular perception of criminal participation could not imagine the benefit of forced confinement.

Post-Revolution

The postrevolutionary world brought new realities. The old forces of socialization were diminishing (Friedman 1993). Immigration and mobility led to anonymity—no longer was the community able to protect itself from outsiders. The dramatic change in the physical and social landscape required new fixes for crime. Although inspired by the Enlightenment (Rothman 1990), the American reformation and professionalism of criminal justice systems were popular endeavors in the republican era (Friedman 1993) because of "the influence of American social conditions, in particular, the fantastic *mobility* of American life" (Friedman 1993, 62, italics in original). Unsocialized and mobile masses bred discomfort. Formal rational fixes seemed reasonable and necessary to local officials and embedded residents. The law itself became a sensible tool for crime prevention: "Americans expected that a rational system of correction, which made punishment certain but humane, would dissuade all but a few offenders from a life of crime" (Rothman 1990, 61). The propositions of deterrence gained in appeal.

Formal state responses did become more attractive. But the intrigue with the primacy of choice in criminal participation did not yet overwhelm environmental theoretical postulations. The law might, in part, reduce criminal participation. But prominent 19th-century perspectives promoted inadequate socialization as the source of crime: "Jacksonians located both the origins of crime and delinquency within the society, with the inadequacies of the family and the unchecked spread of vice through the community" (Rothman 1990, 78). Reformers believed that family disillusionment (Friedman 1993), ineffective schools, increased mobility, and reduced church attendance led to increased criminal involvement (Rothman 1995). This drafted a dilemma: modern society could be blamed for individual transgressions but had not yet developed adequate controls (Friedman 1993). Whipping, shaming, and expulsion were efficient punishments within intimate communities (Friedman 1993), but not within highly populated urban centers. Mobility diminished apprehension, accountability, and socialization (and subsequently increased crime). Within this context of mobile America, a new order of criminal justice thinking and practice emerged that allowed for the birth of the penitentiary through the removal and isolation of the offender (Rothman 1990). Prison could give the offender what society had failed to provide.

The prisons that appeared in the mid-nineteenth century isolated and separated men and women. Reformers "talked about the penitentiary as serving as a model for the family and the school. The prison was nothing less than a 'grand theatre for the trial of all new plans in hygiene and education'" (Rothman 1995, 106). The initial reliance on prison institutions revealed a cultural belief in the power of reformation through reflection and strict routine (see Sutherland, Cressey, and Luckenbill 1992). Prison existed to compassionately fix society's failure: "prison was first regarded as an instrument of humanitarianism . . . prisoners were not to be maltreated. There was food, light, clothing, exercise, ventilation, religious instruction" (Bennett 1970, 70). Two prison models dominated this 19th-century American landscape: Pennsylvania and New York (Auburn).

The Pennsylvania model attempted to empower and reform through fair treatment (without physical abuse). The model was famous for its strict dependence on solitary confinement—absolute isolation and silence (Rothman 1990). Initially, solitary was confined to designated "experiment" areas at the Walnut Street Jail (Bennett 1970, 71); but later it became the central tool of incarceration for prisoners at Cherry Hill (Rothman 1995; Bennett 1970). Pennsylvania endorsed extreme measures to ensure isolation and championed this isolation as the key to successful reform (Rothman 1995). Their rival model in New York contended that prolonged isolation was actually deleterious (Sutherland et al. 1992). Since the Auburn model eventually obtained near universal adoption, it is somewhat ironic that prolonged isolation is still practiced in the United States and still appears to be harmful to those confined (see National Research Council 2014).

Like Pennsylvania, Auburn also promoted silence but allowed prisoners to eat and work together (Bennett 1970; Rothman 1995). And although the rivalry between the Pennsylvania and the New York models was fierce, Rothman (1995, 105) sees the two models as largely promoting the same ideals of "isolation, obedience, and a steady routine of labor." In practice, however, they may have diverged substantially. According to James Bennett (1970, 73), the former director of the Bureau of Prisons, the New York system relied heavily on corporal punishment to ensure compliance: "New York tested the principle of absolute solitary confinement but concluded, 'To make any impression upon convicts there must be suffering.' So New York built the largest penitentiaries in the country and began a reign of terror." It may be difficult to remove retaliatory attitudes toward those who have violated the social compact. But physical abuse undermines altruistic and effective goals of the prison institution. Auburn intended to reform the prisoner through work and reflection. But the use of corporal punishment may have diminished those efforts. In fact, the use of corporal punishment within American prisons was probably more pervasive at this time than is often acknowledged: "the western states set up their prisons as if cruelty was the point of punishment" (Bennett 1970, 75). The "benevolent" intent and purpose of prison are muddied in a practice that induces fear and intimidation.

Post–Civil War

The Pennsylvania model was eventually deserted (Sutherland et al. 1992) and—largely because of economic benefits—the Auburn model prevailed across much of the United States (Rothman 1995; Sutherland et al. 1992). But overcrowding soon made silence an impossible standard to meet (Rothman 1995). And although records of brutal imprisonment practices do exist prior to the Civil War (Bennett 1970), the prison became miserable after the Civil War, "characterized by over-crowding, brutality, and disorder . . . [But it] continued to occupy the central place in criminal punishment" (Rothman 1995, 112). External conditions increased demand and prison managers could not even attempt to meet the ideological intent of the prison institution. But this clear inability did not challenge the utility or the perceived utility of prison:

> Good hearted citizens and generous philanthropists had been appalled at the condition of jails, at the use of corporeal and capital punishment, and had invented the prison to introduce a less cruel and more benevolent mode of punishment. But the difficulty was that, by simply describing the innovation as a reform, historians assumed that the prison was a logical step in the progress of humanity; they failed to ask why the prison was invented in the 1820s and 1830s and why it adopted its special attributes. (Rothman 1995, 114)

It would seem logical that without reason for prison there would be little need for prison. But historical analysis suggests that the prison institution survived even without clear understanding of its purpose. Although more resigned, Friedman (1993, 159) also sees the prison experiment as problematic: "[t]he prison, in general, was a story of failure. . . . Yet there was no going back. Imprisonment was and remained the basic way to punish men and women convicted of serious crimes." The historical consensus is not that the prison institution survived because of its well-conceived and well-understood purpose and impact; instead the prison institution survived because of society's reliance, assumptions, and even indifference. Sutherland et al. (1992, 473) propose that the prison institution may be embedded in the democratic state: "[a]s democracy developed, so did an appreciation of liberty, and restriction of freedom by imprisonment came to be regarded as a proper system for imposing pain on criminals." The esteem with which we hold liberty makes lack of liberty all the more awful. But pain by itself lacks utility. Pain that reduces recidivism, however barbaric, has purpose.

The continued rationale of such a system of punishment—wrought with such contradictions—was not clear. And a prison system that does not clearly define the purpose of punishment through confinement allows for (although does not require) arbitrary and whimsical sentencing practices. As prison changed from a place to await punishment to a place *of* punishment, years became markers of severity:

> The prison sentence was to substitute confinement for execution, and although no records survive that tell us how legislatures initially equated crime with time, it seems likely that their reckonings went from the top down. If murder once brought death, it now brought thirty years. And if murder was worth life, then robbery should bring ten to fifteen years; rape, twelve or fourteen; assault, seven or nine; and burglary six or seven. (Rothman 1995, 113)

Assigning years to crimes is somewhat arbitrary. Additional years of incarceration yield *better* rehabilitation through specific treatment programming; additional years yield *greater* deterrence through empirical realities. But ranking crimes and matching years to crimes combine emotional and objective measures (regardless of future behavior, a murderer is unlikely to receive a short sentence). Without specific empirical fact, year reliance is a retributive measure. This may be a reasonable punishment perspective. But strict reliance on prison years for rehabilitation is unreasonable. And by the start of the 20th century, with rehabilitation as the primary goal of punishment in the United States, indeterminate sentencing helped fashion (at least theoretically) the rationality of the prison stay. Prison stays, in a way, became malleable.

In its purest form, first championed by Alexander Maconochie, indeterminate sentencing considers reform outside of prison years: "sentences should not be for imprisonment for a period of time, but for the performance to be determined and specified quantity of labour; in brief, time sentences should be abolished, and task sentences substituted" (Barry 1956, 151). Maconochie proposed that offenders meet criteria in order to *gain* freedom. The process of imprisonment, moreover, would consist of gaining or losing credit toward release. Maconochie insisted that everything beyond basic sustenance should be earned by the prisoner (see Barry 1956; Bennett 1970). For most of the first half of the 20th century, the United States largely adopted a model of indeterminate sentencing and rehabilitation (MacKenzie 2006). Credit is given to the Irish mark system (Sutherland et al. 1992) as influencing Zebulon Brockway and the model for the Elmira Reformatory; but honoring good behavior and earning one's release from prison was Alexander Maconochie's controversial innovation (Barry 1956; Bennett 1970). There is logic to prison if it targets individuals individually and allows for growth, maturation, and socialization by indicators outside of prison years. This logical system largely ran correctional policy for the first half of the 20th century. But by the 1970s, the American world turned against rehabilitation—nudged sharply by Martinson's (1974) work, rising crime rates, and rising fear of crime. The late twentieth century saw the full impact of this abandonment and the rise of the crime control model and the age of mass incarceration.

Mass Incarceration

Much has been made of the modern US era of mass incarceration (see National Research Council 2014). There are over 2.2 million men and women in US prisons and jails (Glaze and Herberman 2013). Pew Center on the States recently estimated that about 1 in 100 adults is currently incarcerated (2008) and 1 in 31 is currently under some sort of correctional control (Pew Center on the States 2009). This has also been framed as largely a modern phenomenon—six times as large as the early 1970s (Pettit and Western 2004). In fact prior to the 1970s, prison rates were so stable in the United States that some researchers claimed that societies self-regulated their punishment levels in order to maintain constant incarceration rates (Blumstein and Cohen 1973). Blumstein and Cohen (1973) even argued that tumultuous times such as the Great Depression or World War II did not see dramatic changes in the number of incarcerated individuals. Their theoretical discussion speculated that criminal sanctions would change based on the behaviors prevalent during particular times in history. In times of high crime, only the most dangerous and serious offenders would be incarcerated. But in low-crime periods, harsher sanctions would guarantee the equilibrium of the prison system. This conjecture mirrors Durkheim's society of saints, in which crime will exist regardless of local behavior in order to maintain strong societal commitment. Of course, soon after Blumstein and Cohen's (1973) famous declaration, the incarceration rate began to accelerate rapidly and continued to climb for over 30 years. But I contend that their proposition may not have been as foolish as it appears and that the United States may not be in quite as unique a period as some would like to claim. Prior to supporting this claim, I find it necessary to briefly discuss the modern reliance on prison.

Arguably, the dramatic rise in imprisonment over the past three decades may be better explained by a general shift in criminal justice policy rather than any substantial increase in crime (Blumstein and Beck 1999; National Research Council 2014). Captivated not only by Martinson's 1974 infamous claim that rehabilitation did not work, coupled by riots in Chicago, and a theatrical increasing fear of crime—complemented, rationally, by an actual increase in crime—popular culture and criminal justice policy began to scurry quickly toward neoclassical reform (MacKenzie 2006; also see Savelsberg 1992). Prior to its flight of the 1970s, the US criminal justice system championed rehabilitation and individual level theories of punishment (Feeley and Simon 1992). The general perception consisted in fixing the "illness" of offenders. Since the causes of offending were varied, judges utilized discretion in sentencing, meting out punishment case by case, and parole boards reviewed improved offender behavior prior to release (Tonry 2009; 1996). This perspective largely disappeared in the 1970s.

Although the prison buildup often appears to be the perfect confluence of events, Friedman (1993) contends that there is a strong relationship between crime, criminal justice, and culture. Perspectives on crime rise powerfully out of historical times (Friedman 1993). By the early 1970s, the model of indeterminate sentencing came under attack. Detractors from the right claimed that rehabilitation was ineffective—largely using Martinson (1974) as ammunition. Detractors from the left claimed that unfettered discretion in sentencing created massive disparity in the criminal justice system, widely and disproportionately impacting racial minorities (Tonry 1996). Giving voice and clarity to the movement, Frankel (1972) claimed that indeterminate sentencing practices did indeed breed disparity and gave judges too much discretion. Current sentencing practices, Frankel (1972) argued, simultaneously and erroneously assumed not only that judges employ unbounded rationality in decision-making but also that judges bear thorough awareness of the philosophical reasons for punishment. Since this was nearly impossible, Frankel insisted, judges could not possibly be expected to reasonably handle the lofty expectations of indeterminate sentencing while at the same time avoid outcome disparity. Indeed, in the 1970s and 1980s, Federal and State criminal justice systems in the United States began to adopt determinate sentencing practices and a crime control model (Feeley and Simon 1992). But Frankel (1972) also charged that parole was inhumane and that appellate courts needed to review judicial decisions as a safeguard against improper sentencing practices. And by the mid-1980s, parole boards disappeared from the federal system all together (Tonry 1996). Perhaps these attempts were to reduce disparity and increase uniformity of punishment. But it is arguably this shift—away from rehabilitation and indeterminate sentencing—toward determinate sentencing, mandatory minimums, and truth-in-sentencing laws that have greatly contributed to the drastic increases in imprisonment in the United States (MacKenzie 2002; Blumstein and Beck 1999).

Young and Brown (1993) assert that the swelling of prison populations is due to both the increase in the length of sentences and the increase in the number of admissions while the decrease in prison populations is primarily an issue of addressing sentence length (see also Blumstein and Beck 1999). In order to effectively locate the reasons for prison augmentation, thereby, it is necessary to target two areas: particular increases in sanctions that would result in longer sentences, and increases in certain types of prison admissions that might begin to detail how the prison population exploded so dramatically. In partial answer to this, Blumstein and Beck (1999) claim that drug offending is responsible for 45% of the total growth in the incarceration rate over the past 30 years. The increase in the States was primarily due to an increase in drug arrests and commitment to prison—and not to increases in sentencing (Blumstein and Beck 1999). The increase in the federal system, however, was a product of increases in average prison stays, an increase in arrest rates, *and* an increase in commitment rates (Blumstein and Beck 1999). It also is possible that the thespian War on Drugs of the 1980s—which raised the penalty on crack possession, among other things—largely increased the actual number of individuals arrested for possession and simultaneously sentenced those same individuals to longer prison stays (Caplow and Simon 1999). Drug arrests, in fact, might be somewhat controversial. Ruth and Reitz (2003) contend that as overall arrest rates remain constant (or decline) then the percentage of drug crimes actually increases. Indeed, this suggests that policing might play a critical role in the production of arrest rates, especially in stagnant times. Violent and property crimes require police to *react* whereas police may *proactively* detain drug addicts from known locales in the city. Subsequently, Ruth and Reitz (2003) note that over 80% of all drug arrests are for possession. All in all, it is feasible that the changing climate in the criminal justice system—away from rehabilitation and toward control (MacKenzie 2002)—coupled with the increased penalties for drug crimes, resulted in harsher sentencing practices and eventually created the massive incarceration rates we witness today.

But these policies have not impacted citizens of the United States equally. The likelihood of imprisonment is far greater for the uneducated and for people of color. Recent estimates suggest that close to 70% of black men who failed to complete high school spent one year in prison by the time they reached their mid-30s (Pettit 2012). The disproportionate number of urban, poor, black males in prison suggests that mass incarceration may be more adequately described as "hyper incarceration" (Wacquant 2010; see also Sampson and Loeffler 2010). Sampson and Loeffler (2010) further demonstrate that, irrespective of crime rate, neighborhood disadvantage substantially drives incarceration rates. While these dismal trends appear to be modern phenomena, forced institutionalization of US citizens may be consistent with historical practice. Indeed, our current institutionalization rates might not be a modern phenomenon. If one includes mental hospitals as a form of incarceration, then the United States actually incarcerates similar levels per capita as compared to the 1950s (Harcourt 2011). This does not indicate that mental patients now inhabit prisons instead of asylums. But it does suggest that US policy has a much cozier relationship with institutionalization, or the formal restriction of freedom, than modern apologists would have one believe. In fact, this offers mild vindication for Blumstein and Cohen (1973). This should not excuse or justify current incarceration rates. But it might help to provide a larger context of policy, both current and historical.

The need for institutionalization may be important for the American lifestyle. Today, we allow the prison industry to excessively and disproportionately target poor men of color. I believe that it would be remiss to discuss prison management without this broader context, without considering the composition of prisoners and the policies that have contributed to create the current conditions that trouble US corrections. Prison workers oversee populations that US policy deems unfit to live unsupervised lives. It would be reckless to assume that the unique and specific composition of this population plays no role in the experience of being a prison worker and of working in a prison institution.

THE BUREAU OF PRISONS

Although three federal prisons were constructed in the late 1800s to address the rising population of federal detainees, these institutions "operated virtually autonomously" (Roberts 1997, 53) and it was not until the 1930s that the US government officially approved the establishment of the Bureau of Prisons (BOP). The passage of the Three Prisons Act in 1891 gave the federal government direct oversight of its prisoners but it did little to ensure coherent and central oversight or consistent treatment and practice across its institutions (DiIulio 1991a; Bennett 1970; Roberts 1997). Indeed, early oversight of federal facilities was minimal. Inmate conditions were deplorable, unsanitary—even inhumane. Weak central authority proved unable to provide effective and meaningful management: "haphazard administration of federal prisons and the lack of central direction inhibited federal prisons from responding effectively to advances in correctional philosophy" (Roberts 1997, 53). In the 1920s, prohibition dramatically increased the number of federal prisoners and overcrowding became a real concern. To address these endemic inadequacies, President Hoover signed into law the creation of BOP in 1930 and gave oversight to a strong central authority (Roberts 1997; DiIulio 1991a).

The early leadership of the Bureau of Prisons advocated for rehabilitation. The first BOP director was Sanford Bates, an effective manager who tactfully organized and professionalized the bureau: "Bates's contribution was immense. He took his stand . . . on the assumption that either our social structure is hopelessly maladjusted or there must be causes that can be ascertained for the incidence of crime. He believed criminality could be cured in medical fashion and that punishment of criminals was out of date" (Bennett 1970, 86). Likewise James Bennett—Bates's successor and director for close to 30 years—was a reformer. Bennett envisioned imprisonment through rehabilitation; he saw prison as an institution whose legitimacy could only thrive and whose methods could only be effective if its humanity could not be questioned. Bennett (1970) hailed key progressive reformers of sensible and humane prison practices as his influences: Alexander Maconochie, Zebulon Brockway, and Thomas Mott Osborne. All three men were pioneers in prison practices that demanded fair treatment of prisoners and abhorred cruelty and brutality. True to form, when he later was appointed director of BOP, Bennett's (1970, 91) first official act was to abolish the nightstick: "I knew that corporal punishment was not allowed in federal prisons but also that it was secretly practiced, and that the nightstick was in fact the symbol of punitive authority."

Bennett was an influential voice prior to and during his tenure as director. Prior to the establishment of the BOP, Bennett had argued for the creation of a federal prison bureau with the goal to "humanize prison life" and—ironically, given the federal government's subsequent view of narcotics—he had called on that bureau to "build three new penitentiaries and experimental-type institutions, also two new 'narcotics' farms in which addicts could be treated separately from the rest of the prison population" (Bennett 1970, 84). In addition, Bennett (1970, 84) had advised that "the emphasis of prison reform ought to be placed on work." He believed that offenders could be reformed and that drug addicts were sick—and needed treatment. The bureau largely heeded Bennett's early advice. In 1934, BOP launched Federal Prison Industries (FPI), which ensured that work would be central to each prisoner's federal imprisonment (Roberts 1997; Bennett 1970). But Bennett was neither naïve nor unfamiliar with the prison institution, having witnessed great brutality in American prisons (then championed as effective punishment techniques). His complex perspective on the intention of prison was impressive: "one misjudgment—and prison reform loses ground in a community. One man released from prison too soon might mean a woman raped or a bank held up at gunpoint. One man released from prison too late might mean a hopeful individual turned manic-depressive, useless to society, and a perpetrator of much more serious, violent crime" (Bennett 1970, 44). Per Bennett, prison stays could be too short *and* too long. But the sole purpose of the prison institution revolved around rehabilitation and successful reintegration. External pressures would make this a much more difficult reality to fulfill in the latter part of the 20th century.

The size of the inmate population today in the Bureau of Prisons is largely reflective of policies over the past 30 years and not a gradual increase over the last 80 years: "for the first five decades of BOP's existence, the number of prisons and the number of inmates remained fairly stable . . . by the mid-1980s, however, intensified prosecution of drug laws, the introduction of sentencing guidelines, and the discontinuation of federal parole created a period of unprecedented growth in the BOP" (Roberts 1997, 54). The punishment philosophy that was envisioned by Bates and Bennett evaporated in the American landscape. Modern policies directly challenged those promoted by the bureau's founding directors. Rehabilitation perspectives gave way to crime control perspectives. Labor to control populations by keeping them busy is not the same as providing skills to enable crime-free futures. Forces outside the prison community restricted options for the bureau. Even though work and skill advancement are still a critical component of the bureau's mission, dissolving parole arguably challenged the incentive structure.

BOP currently houses over 217,000 inmates in 117 prisons (Samuels 2014). As late as 1980, the total Federal inmate population was only 24,242—spread out across 24 institutions. Each of the two concluding decades of the 20th century saw the federal inmate population more than double—once in the 1980s and again in the 1990s. At the close of the 20th century close to 140,000 inmates were in federal custody (USDOJ 2011). Most of the growth is credited to increases in the use of mandatory sentencing and the Sentencing Reform Act of 1984 (USDOJ 2011). Notably, the Sentencing Reform Act abolished parole, directed the newly formed US Sentencing Commission to develop federal sentencing guidelines—or determinate sentencing—and dramatically limited judicial discretion. Consequently, a sizeable amount of this growth is due to the changing practices in the sentencing of drug offenders (Blumstein and Beck 1999). Of those currently serving sentences in federal prison, 48.2% are drug offenders. Weapons offenders—including arson and explosives—the next largest detained population account for only 15.9% of the overall prison population (Bureau of Prisons 2012). This does not appear to reflect the vision espoused by Bennett.

PRIORITY AND PURPOSE

Prioritizing Safety in Prison

The National Research Council ([NRC] 2014) recently advised, in a published report, that current national incarceration rates are essentially unjustifiable. The evidence suggests that the goals of punishment are not being met and that the social costs are unreasonably high. The policy implication is decarceration. Dramatic reductions in prison populations should result in a change in inmate composition—whereby more dangerous individuals remain incarcerated and less dangerous or low-risk men and women are diverted to alternative corrections initiatives. Given the summation by the NRC—and with an eye to the future—it is reasonable for corrections managers and corrections researchers to anticipate (or at least consider) this potential shift in prisoner composition. Within this world, security and safety of prisoners and prison staff need to remain the priority—without exception or distraction. Importantly, changing sentencing strategies (relying more on alternatives to incarceration) will change the demographic of the prison population but should also come with a clear intention of imprisonment, and this intention should come from civil society. Throughout this book, I largely contend that civil society should clearly define prison intention *and* prison philosophy and that prison will be successful if it consistently and fairly meets those definitions. Fair treatment is consistent and predictable. It is not necessarily what the prisoner wants but what the prisoner can reasonably expect. And the prisoner should expect prison to be focused primarily on security and safety. The more dangerous the population, the more necessary this goal.

Although it is reasonable and appropriate to prioritize security as the primary goal of prison, this does not suggest that security measures are applied without regulation, oversight, or supervision. But it does demand that the safety of prisoners and prison staff are essential. The rhetoric that clouds and even challenges this priority is often clever: "there can be too much emphasis on 'security values,' at the expense of other values. This orientation includes security procedures but also includes a position taken towards prisoners, that casts them as not to be trusted, as threatening and deserving of punishment" (Liebling 2004, 441). De-emphasizing security is inappropriate and Liebling conflates two separate processes: formal control of the institution and bias toward prisoner populations. It is reasonable to assume that prisoners are indeed deserving of punishment (given that the state has sentenced them to confinement) *and* not brutalize them. It is reasonable in that most individuals perceive the loss of freedom as a significant and sufficient price to pay (Sutherland et al. 1992). Imprisonment does not require additional pain for it to be a punishing experience. I admit that those who are not dangerous and therefore not threatening may not need to be in prison—and very likely should not be in prison. But if the purpose of prison is to remove those who are unable to abide by the collective will (and are indeed dangerous) then how is it unreasonable for prison workers to hold the very same perspectives that the public holds? Unless this perspective necessarily leads to brutality, harboring reasonable bias that is not acted on through biased rule application is not problematic. To avoid misinterpretation, I do strongly support the National Research Council's (2014, 329) assertion: "the principle of citizenship requires that the punishment of prison should not be so severe that it causes damage to prisoners, places them at serious risk of significant harm, or compromises their chances to lead a fulfilling and successful life after they are released." The nuance that I propose is for the prison to exert the least amount of formal control possible while maintaining security and safety as the primary objectives of that exerted action. This implores prison administrators to employ empirical research and risk assessment tools in order to adequately apply formal control.

Prison administrators are not faced with the choice to *either* generate a civil (or democratic) prison society *or* brutalize prisoners. This is a false dichotomy. I believe that corrections researchers understand this but fail to clearly promote prison priority and prison intention and therefore occasionally present potentially misunderstood claims. Liebling's (2004) general position appears to perceive substantial overlap between the fabric of civil society and prison society. Yet progressive civil society aims to protect individual lives, to allow for freedom in self-directed pursuits, and to protect against arbitrary government interference. Civil society is a place to *join* and to *remain*. Imprisonment, however, is a result of the failure to abide by the regulations of civil society. Certainly, it is logical to attempt to impose or instill values of civil society onto imprisoned men and women (in an attempt to assimilate them or prepare them for their release). But imprisonment is a place to transition *out of*—a place to leave and not return. I do not understand Liebling to discount the importance of security within prisons. She illustrates a rather thoughtful and intricate reality:

> [P]risons are special communities . . . which exist at once outside and inside social community. Their form is shaped by social and political ideas held about crime, punishment, social order, and human nature. Many of the practices within them are also shaped by these ideas. Prisoners are generally held against their will. In this sense, but also in others, prisons suffer from an "inherent legitimacy deficit." They are not consensual communities; and as such, they are susceptible to abuses of power and to breakdowns in order. (Liebling 2004, 462)

In part, I take this excerpt as an admonition of state power. Indeed, imprisonment is a remarkably profound exercise in state power, and imprisonment should be limited to only dangerous individuals. But she also appears to advocate for the modification of prison institutions to make them more reasonable to those who are incarcerated: "The question remains, is it possible to construct a form of imprisonment whose basic structure and daily practices are more or less acceptable to those who endure it, despite their domination and commonly low social position?" (Liebling 2004, 491). I agree that brutal and cruel prisons are unacceptable. But happy prisoners are not an appropriate goal. Of course, I do not believe this is Liebling's point. But if this is not her argument then what is really "acceptable" for an imprisoned individual? The answer must return to fair and consistent treatment. And I believe this is Liebling's intent. But since I fail to see how the really disturbing reality of prison is not forced confinement itself—the prison cell, a decidedly inflexible component—I am led to conclude that reasonable and acceptable confinement parameters are better designed by the civil state and not by those who may (and probably *should*) view the basic condition of confinement as unacceptable. This emphasis is integral.

Admittedly, the greater issue is that confinement itself is a moral problem and yet our own humanity gives us little recourse beyond it. If civil society defines normative behavior (and this may often be faulty) then civil society should also define appropriate punishment for violation of codified law— including the conditions within places of punishment. Unless the state is willing to liberally apply capital punishment, then intermediate sanctions, namely imprisonment, are necessary. But, at the minimum, those who have demonstrated their willingness to harm should not be allowed to continue to demonstrate their willingness to harm once incarcerated. I do not see how this standard can be logically sidestepped. This requires that those incarcerated do not inflict harm on other prisoners or on prison staff. And this requires that security and safety are the first and most important conditions of imprisonment. I do not suggest that perception is unimportant. Perceived legitimacy and humane treatment likely contribute to the effectiveness of security and safety preservation.

BOP arguably shares the perspective that security and safety are paramount. Although BOP adopts seven specific goals for operation, safety and security are integral to the first goal (and arguably the priority): "*the BOP will proactively manage its offender population to ensure safe and secure operations*" (USDOJ 2009, 2, italics in original). In addition, BOP strives for "humane correctional services" (USDOJ 2010, 1) but not for democratic civil society. Prison management can work. US prisons saw a dramatic decrease in violence and chaos through strong leadership, strict security focus, and order maintenance (Useem and Goldstone 2002; Useem and Piehl 2006). Ultimately, reducing the number of those who enter prison is a more logical solution than challenging (or coyly undermining) the supreme importance of security. I do concede, however, that perhaps Liebling's (2004) position is appropriate for European prisons. But the United States is unique in its violent crime rates and its incarceration rates. And if we begin to shift prison admission toward violent offenders—and away from nonviolent offenders— then we also change overall prisoner composition. This will further demand that the safety and security of all those in prison, by choice or by force, are not jeopardized.

Punishment Philosophy and Prison Workers

The burden of prisons further increases when considered in relation to the philosophy of punishment. Theoretically, the purpose of incarceration is to serve an end goal. The presumption: society rationally detains men and women. The prevalence and dominance of crime control models throughout the latter part of the 20th century illustrated a punitive American culture, convinced by the utility of deterrence and incapacitation (see National Research Council 2014). Today, America is more nuanced. The end of the twentieth century saw rehabilitation reborn. In fact, research suggested that rehabilitation could work (Cullen and Gendreau 2000; MacKenzie 2006; Andrews and Bonta 2006). Current economic conditions have arguably convinced even the staunchest proponents of extravagant crime control measures that alternatives to incarceration are warranted (see Gest 2014; Strand 2012). Undoubtedly, the focus on "what works" has gained steam. But the overall goal of incarceration, nonetheless, is not always clear. Rehabilitation has not *replaced* incapacitation or deterrence. And we do not so easily promote a clear rationale for imprisonment:

> Traditionally, Americans have wanted a criminal justice apparatus that apprehends and visits harm upon the guilty, makes offenders more law-abiding and virtuous, dissuades would-be offenders from criminal pursuits, invites most convicts to return to the bosom of the community, and achieves these ends in a civilized and financially manageable way. (DiIulio 1987, 259)

Demanding divergent goals of punishment within one facility might be impractical and self-serving. But it also increases the burden for prison workers. If we are unclear about the purpose of prison or we make demands that are unreasonable given the limitations of the prison institution, then we generate an impossible demand for prison workers. If we expect prisons to simultaneously incapacitate, rehabilitate, deter, and avenge—and the prescribed punishment depends on the particulars of the offender—then we ask correctional officers to swallow a certain amount of complexity in order to effectively complete daily tasks. Of course, this proposition could be averted if prisons themselves met these diverse outcomes without the knowledge of, or without assistance from, the prison worker. But even line-staff correctional officers play a significant role in effectively managing the day-to-day operations of the prison institution. Failure to understand meaning in orders may reduce the likelihood that orders are prioritized. Divergent goals of prison punishment are worthwhile but they do appear to require line-staff commitment. I submit that if prisons are to successfully meet diverse goals then the collective endeavor of prison itself needs to promote an institutional culture that elevates the importance of the individual in the eyes of the community.

The contribution of the individual, in this sense, is promoted as it furthers the collective goal of the prison. Institutional goals are met by individual cooperation. Undermining the role of the individual within this system may be detrimental to institutional goals.

Unfortunately, the prescriptions of prison work itself create ambiguity. Rather than actively target prisoners as Goffman (1961) implied, it is plausible that prison workers who subscribe to institutional code more frequently ignore or disregard prisoners. The job itself concerns self-survival, evading blame, and minimizing disruption. In this light, the charges become objects to move, to feed. The future may only increase this relational distance. Increases in technology, specifically in adopted surveillance measures, may reduce gross physical violations. But technology is unlikely to impact neglect and indifference. And yet, this outcome is not necessarily problematic: it may even improve prison worker job satisfaction and effectiveness. Yes, this is a controversial perspective. I am suggesting that a *type* of dehumanization may be beneficial to the prison worker. This proposition suggests that dehumanization exists on a dissociation *spectrum* with a beneficial and tame end—namely, objectivity (generally reserved for occupations such as clinical psychology or therapy). This contention does not require that correctional officers view prisoners as cattle. Rather, it suggests that emotional investment may undermine the ability of prison workers to successfully complete their work. Emotional investment clouds rational, objective, and consistent oversight. Just because the worker is emotionally removed from the subject does not demand that she is also unable to witness abuse or pain or need. Therefore, meaning for the prison worker may be generated by prisoner oversight but should be reinforced through supervisory accolade. While disconnect from prisoners may be advantageous, disconnect from supervisors may be counterproductive for institutional goals.

Keep in mind that correctional officers are asked to oversee antisocial populations that have formally expressed lack of concern for the social order and to do so without bias and without emotion. Clearly, this is an ideal setting for alienation from work, from peers, and from charges. And it is likely that different settings, even those operating on the same mission statements and overall code of conduct, could understand and employ power in largely divergent fashions. It is also likely, however, that highly centralized prison systems like the US Bureau of Prisons may have less variation across prisons. Therefore, this is not merely a question of institutional variation but also what types of factors—within and across prisons—promote commitment, improve inmate management, and reduce emotional hardening of prison workers. This is not a contradiction. In this context, emotional hardening suggests that the emotional investment of prison work has taken a great toll. The work itself has desensitized and engulfed the worker. The prison worker is asked to maintain objectivity without becoming overwhelmed by reality. He is asked to reserve judgment and to emotionally disconnect himself from a population that is highly disadvantaged, needy, and antisocial. This is an incredibly difficult task that I argue requires strong institutional and peer support. Emotional distance from the prisoner may be advantageous but emotional hardening implies a profound environmental effect on the worker and is not advantageous. Both could be considered forms of dehumanization but I argue that emotional distance is appropriate and emotional hardening is detrimental. In this work, I target the detrimental form of dehumanization—which directly costs both the worker and the prisoner. The worker perceives the prisoner as an object and the worker subjects himself to great emotional fatigue. I fundamentally ask, therefore, what role can and does prison management play in the promotion of power, the advancement of prisoner oversight, and the reduction of dehumanization?

Security and Purpose

It is a nonnegotiable condition that security is the most important goal of prison management. But punishment itself needs to be considered as existing on a spectrum (see Morris and Tonry 1990). The goal of punishment is not to create one institution that can best meet the myriad of social goals for a variety of dissimilar offenders—but rather to tailor treatment toward treatable populations, deterrence toward deterrable populations (see Piquero and Pogarsky 2002; Pogarsky 2002; Pogarsky and Piquero 2003), retribution toward populations that horrify the public, and incapacitation toward populations that cannot seem to cease chronic offending. In this way it is neither a goal of creating nor promoting the best institution given massive restrictions (as DiIulio arguably does); instead, the goal is to create the best institutions given the limitations and strengths of particular offending populations. The goal of retribution, for example, may be ill-suited for an institution that has become a coming-of-age experience for black youth (see Pettit and Western 2004; National Research Council 2014). But if prisoners leave prison as offenders, then prison is failing. Given the negligible impact of prison on rehabilitation and as a specific deterrent (Nagin et al. 2009), this may be the case. But rehabilitation can work (MacKenzie 2006). Either the current use or design of prison, therefore, appears unable to meet offender needs.

I do reason that it is possible for prisons to reflect our moral prohibitions and yet still comply with our standards of morality: they are not mutually exclusive. Just as "legal sanctions serve to reinforce our notion of morality" (Paternoster 2010, 56), our same morality demands that prisons uphold the most basic of human protection. But this proposition is intricate. Prison standards do not reflect our perceived morality but our actual morality.

While criminal sanctions reflect our notion of morality, prison conditions and imprisonment practices reflect our active morality. Therefore, we must answer for the mass imprisonment of the poor and of uneducated men of color (National Research Council 2014). I infer, perhaps unfairly, that the superficial subscription to multiple goals of prison specifically protects us from this harsh and unjustifiable reality. Proven reductions in recidivism rates for those released from prison will help release this tension and justify our adoption of punishment goals outside of incapacitation.

Fortunately, it is possible that newer penal managers no longer consider the success or failure of ex-prisoners as irrelevant to the operation of prisons: "Correctional managers are no longer distancing themselves from what happens after release. In fact, quite the contrary—many are embracing it as one of their major goals" (Petersilia 2003, 252). The federal government has taken great interest in predatory behaviors within prisons (Fellner 2010) and in those reentering society (National Research Council 2014). Progressive and effective reentry services are appearing in multiple states (see National Research Council 2014). Research and policy are challenging reporting practices for ex-offenders (Decker et al. 2014). Indeed, the successful adoption of a reentry perspective may alter the prison environment by diverting future inmates to alternative sentences and by systematically dividing those we are mad at from those whom we fear. Yet, security measures may be even more important as prisoner composition changes. Prisoners will still be released and prison managers may need to consider how to improve implementation and integration of adequate treatment services and programs without compromising safety. Fundamentally, current prison ubiquity may overreach societal need. Although security must be the primary goal of prison management, this goal does not assume (or demand) that all offenders must therefore be placed in prison.

Chapter 3

Analytic Method

This chapter details the general analytic strategy employed in this book. For those interested in the statistical approach used for analysis, this chapter will be beneficial and informative. However, less technical readers may be willing to advance to Chapter 4. Detailed information regarding the selected sample, the analytic strategy, and the precise strategy of variable construction are provided here. General descriptive information about variables of particular interest is also provided in this chapter (see Tables 3.1 and 3.2).

SAMPLE

This study employs data from the Federal Bureau of Prisons (BOP) yearly Prison Social Climate Survey (PSCS). The BOP utilizes a stratified proportional probability sample design and selects survey participants from each BOP correctional institution in the United States (Saylor 2006). Proportional probability helps to maximize the likelihood that staff at each facility is represented in proportion to sex, race, occupational specialty, and supervisory status (Saylor 2006). Responses to the survey for calendar years 2006–2010 are as follows:

Year 2006: 9,021 (70.9% response rate)
Year 2007: 9,298 (71.3% response rate)
Year 2008: 7,997 (65.3% response rate)
Year 2009: 9,596 (59.9% response rate)
Year 2010: 10,058 (59.8% response rate)

Table 3.1   Descriptive Statistics for Primary Predictors and Outcomes

	Mean	SD	Min	Max
2007				
Institutional Commitment (n = 4522)	0.0	1.00	−2.55	1.57
Efficacy (n = 4464)	0.0	1.00	−3.35	2.04
Hardening (n = 4455)	0.0	1.00	−1.80	2.88
Alienation (n = 4281)	0.0	1.00	−2.26	4.12
Normlessness (n = 4406)	0.0	1.00	−1.78	3.93
Powerlessness (n = 4495)	0.0	1.00	−2.20	2.09
Meaninglessness (n = 4469)	0.0	1.00	−2.07	2.94
Isolation (n = 4458)	0.0	1.00	−1.68	4.40
Estrangement (n = 4544)	0.0	1.00	−1.24	3.06
Legitimate Power (n = 4468)	0.0	1.00	−2.94	1.50
Referent Power (n = 4424)	0.0	1.00	−2.38	1.69
Expert Power (n = 4499)	0.0	1.00	−2.93	1.62
Reward Power (n = 4528)	0.0	1.00	−1.22	1.74
Coercive Power (n = 4497)	0.0	1.00	−0.72	2.89
2008				
Institutional Commitment (n = 3796)	0.0	1.00	−2.57	1.57
Efficacy (n = 3729)	0.0	1.00	−3.35	2.05
Hardening (n = 3714)	0.0	1.00	−1.81	2.92
Alienation (n = 2352)	0.0	1.00	−1.99	1.67
Normlessness (n = 3332)	0.0	1.00	−1.70	4.06
Powerlessness (n = 3768)	0.0	1.00	−2.21	2.06
Meaninglessness (n = 3748)	0.0	1.00	−2.03	2.98
Isolation (n = 2471)	0.0	1.00	−1.34	4.81
Estrangement (n = 3826)	0.0	1.00	−1.26	3.11
Legitimate Power (n = 3729)	0.0	1.00	−2.83	1.48
Referent Power (n = 3715)	0.0	1.00	−2.37	1.70
Expert Power (n = 3786)	0.0	1.00	−2.86	1.62
Reward Power (n = 3787)	0.0	1.00	−1.29	1.67
Coercive Power (n = 3763)	0.0	1.00	−0.74	2.83
2009				
Institutional Commitment (n = 4410)	0.0	1.00	−2.56	1.56
Efficacy (n = 4353)	0.0	1.00	−3.46	1.96
Hardening (n = 4383)	0.0	1.00	−1.80	3.01
Alienation (n = 2995)	0.0	1.00	−2.12	4.12
Normlessness (n = 3089)	0.0	1.00	−1.68	3.82
Powerlessness (n = 4436)	0.0	1.00	−2.01	2.18
Meaninglessness (n = 3151)	0.0	1.00	−1.96	3.04
Isolation (n = 3115)	0.0	1.00	−1.54	4.25
Estrangement (n = 4454)	0.0	1.00	−1.17	3.28
Legitimate Power (n = 4404)	0.0	1.00	−2.94	1.50
Referent Power (n = 3107)	0.0	1.00	−2.38	1.69
Expert Power (n = 4431)	0.0	1.00	−2.93	1.62
Reward Power (n = 4484)	0.0	1.00	−1.22	1.74
Coercive Power (n = 4462)	0.0	1.00	−0.72	2.89

Table 3.1 (cont.)

	Mean	SD	Min	Max
2010				
Institutional Commitment (n = 4619)	0.0	1.00	−2.64	1.50
Efficacy (n = 4503)	0.0	1.00	−3.65	1.93
Hardening (n = 4502)	0.0	1.00	−1.77	3.01
Alienation (n = 4317)	0.0	1.00	−2.04	4.26
Normlessness (n = 4571)	0.0	1.00	−1.68	4.04
Powerlessness (n = 4656)	0.0	1.00	−1.97	2.23
Meaninglessness (n = 4623)	0.0	1.00	−1.84	3.15
Isolation (n = 4665)	0.0	1.00	−1.56	4.04
Estrangement (n = 4654)	0.0	1.00	−1.13	3.42
Legitimate Power (n = 4598)	0.0	1.00	−3.34	1.34
Referent Power (n = 4615)	0.0	1.00	−2.54	1.56
Expert Power (n = 4681)	0.0	1.00	−3.20	1.40
Reward Power (n = 4713)	0.0	1.00	−1.47	1.52
Coercive Power (n = 4664)	0.0	1.00	−0.67	2.83

Source: Data from the Prison Social Climate Survey, Federal Bureau of Prisons, 2007–2010.

Institutions with fewer than 120 staff members are fully sampled. Larger facilities, those with staff exceeding 400, are 30% sampled. Institutions that fall in-between 120 and 400 staff members are sampled at their percentage relative to 120 as the marker for fully sampled (Saylor 2006). Participants for the PSCS are selected from those institutions that have been operating for at least six months. Survey questions largely require correctional workers to consider conditions over the past six months. According to BOP: "all employees are 'correctional workers first.' This means everyone is responsible for the security and good order of the institution" (USDOJ 2011, 4). It is therefore appropriate to include all prison workers in this inquiry. Supervisory position and specific occupational role within the prison will be considered in model construction. The inclusion of all workers improves the sample size and variance of outcomes. More importantly, if all workers are trained as correctional officers, first there is little theoretical reason for omitting certain types of officers. I do, however, control for line officers (e.g., correctional officers) in all statistical models. I admit that it is possible that the line officer's experiences after training may differ from other prison workers' experiences.

Four versions of the PSCS exist and are randomly assigned to the sampled populations within institutions. This permits a broader range of pursuits for the comprehension of organizational climate (Saylor 1984). All respondents answer general demographic and occupational questions relating to work assignments, inmate contact, and BOP tenure. Due to random assignment, aggregations of certain measures that do not appear across all four versions of surveys (likely appearing in only two of the four) are used as markers of

Table 3.2 Descriptive Statistics for Select Institutional Level Variables and HLM Unconditional Models (variation across prisons by dependent variable by year)

Descriptive Statistics for Institutional Level Variables				
	Number of Institutions	Mean	SD	Min	Max
2006					
Supervision	114	3.60	0.32	2.85	4.73
Orientation	114	2.17	0.22	1.61	2.84
Fear	114	2.10	0.61	0.192	4
Prison Age	114	24.35	24.34	1	111
2007					
Supervision	116	3.62	0.31	2.70	4.27
Orientation	116	2.14	0.23	1.45	2.81
Fear	116	2.07	0.67	0.58	3.87
Prison Age	116	24.29	23.94	1	112
2008					
Supervision	116	3.67	0.36	2.65	4.68
Orientation	116	2.13	0.24	1.28	2.8
Fear	116	2.20	0.73	0.42	3.88
Prison Age	116	25.96	24.31	2	113
2009					
Supervision	115	3.76	0.34	2.97	4.50
Orientation	115	2.12	0.20	1.57	2.71
Fear	115	1.95	0.73	0.11	4.01
Prison Age	115	27.16	24.39	0	114

HLM Unconditional Models		
	Efficacy	Institutional Commitment	Hardening
2007	$\tau00 = 0.02619$, $p < 0.001$	$\tau00 = 0.15019$, $p < 0.001$	$\tau00 = 0.02998$, $p < 0.001$
2008	$\tau00 = 0.03947$, $p < 0.001$	$\tau00 = 0.14325$, $p < 0.001$	$\tau00 = 0.02536$, $p < 0.001$
2009	$\tau00 = 0.04031$, $p < 0.001$	$\tau00 = 0.12142$, $p < 0.001$	$\tau00 = 0.03365$, $p < 0.001$
2010	$\tau00 = 0.01996$, $p < 0.001$	$\tau00 = 0.12358$, $p < 0.001$	$\tau00 = 0.03571$, $p < 0.001$

Source: Data from the PSCS, Federal Bureau of Prisons, 2006–2009.

institutional level averages. This allows one to control for differences in institutional-average attitudes (e.g., toward supervision or training) across institutions. Since the selection of sampled populations is random within selected demographics and the selection of version for that sampled respondent is also random, this is not problematic. Due to this sampling design, it is also possible to infer institutional demographic percentages by populations sampled. Since PSCS is a stratified sample by gender and race, it can be reasonably inferred that percentages of female respondents by institution reflect that institution's percentage of female staff members. Notably, every operating prison in the BOP is sampled each year in the PSCS. This provides for a full population of prisons for the purpose of level-2 analysis for each surveyed year.

ANALYTIC STRATEGY

I estimate a series of hierarchical linear models (HLM) for the three dependent measures: efficacy, institutional commitment, and hardening (see Tables 4.1 and 5.1). Hierarchical modeling is particularly useful in the context of prisons since it tackles potential bias due to the clustered nature of the observations. HLM is also able to address important group level variability. Differences in group means are likely to influence primary outcomes. In addition, HLM allows for analysis of cross-level interaction (the interaction of security level with key predictors is of particular interest). The level-1 unconditional model for prison workers is understood by the following equation:

$$Y_{ij} = \beta_{0j} + r_{ij}$$

where, β_{0j} is the mean and r_{ij} is the individual observational distance from the mean. At level-2 of the unconditional model, the following equation is adopted:

$$\beta_{0j} = y_{00} + u_{0j}$$

where, β_{0j} is equal to the grand mean (y_{00}) plus a random error term (u_{0j}) that captures un-modeled variability between prisons (the observational distance between individual prisons and the grand mean of all prisons). The full equation with substitution is:

$$Y_{ij} = y_{00} + u_{0j} + r_{ij}$$

This model offers insight into the proportion of the outcome variable that can be explained by differences between prisons, or the intraclass correlation coefficient (ICC), and whether variation between prisons is significant. The ICC is computed by dividing the level-2 variance by the sum of the level-1 and level-2 variance. Reduction in variance (level-1 and level-2) from the initial unconditional model to later specified models can also serve to provide an estimate for the amount of variance explained due to included predictors. This is similar to the r-squared in ordinary least squares regression. Proportion of explained variance in specified models, compared to unconditional models, is noted. All outcomes show significant variation at the institutional level and therefore warrant multilevel modeling techniques. It is important to note however that the variables "Efficacy" and "Hardening" demonstrate that only about 3–4% of the variation is at the institutional level. Due to the strong central authority of the BOP, this is not surprising. Nevertheless, institutional level analysis does not corrupt the individual level analysis and the conclusions that can be drawn on the individual level remain robust. In addition, the analysis demonstrates that for the variable "Institutional Commitment" about 12–15% of total variation is at the institutional level. Using the HLM statistical package to verify these findings, unconditional models are first estimated (Table 3.2). Results indicate significant variation across prisons by dependent variable.

After the initial empty model, further specified models estimate the impact of individual level measures without institutional level variables in order to ascertain continued relevance of multilevel models when the model is fully specified at level-1 (random intercept models with only level-1 predictors). Primary predictors are next modeled against outcome variables and tested for slope variation across institutions. Hypothesis testing is employed to assess improved model fit of the fixed versus the random slope model.

Controlling for the before-listed individual (level-1) and prison level measures (level-2), fully specified models next estimate the impact of primary predictors on primary dependent variables. Random intercept models are specified as follows:

$$Y_{ij} = \beta_{0j} + \beta_{1j}X_{ij} + r_{ij}$$

$$\beta_{0j} = y_{00} + y_{01}Z + u_{0j}$$

$$\beta_{ij} = y_{10}$$

$$Y_{ij} = y_{00} + y_{10}X_{ij} + y_{01}Z + u_{0j} + r_{ij}$$

where, Xs represent individual level variables (level-1), Zs represent institutional level variables (level-2), and variance is explained at the individual and at the prison level. In order to specify random coefficient models—where level-1 variables are permitted to vary across prisons—an additional random effect is specified: $\beta_{ij} = y_{10} + u_{1j}$. If, for example, legitimate power is permitted to vary across institutions, u_{1j} would capture this variation. Notably, all models utilize restricted maximum likelihood (REML) with robust standard errors in HLM. This strategy is employed due to lower reliabilities (Wooldredge, Griffin, and Pratt 2001) and correction for bias in standard errors.

FACTOR ANALYSIS

Dependent and independent variables are constructed through principal component factor analysis. Each developed measure loads sufficiently onto a single factor. Items that sufficiently load onto single factors have only a single Eigenvalue over 1. Generally, this value is close to or above a value of 2. The correlation of individual variables to the factor (see Tables 4.1 and 5.1) and the percentage of total observed variance explained by the factor is also addressed.

SPECIFICS OF MODEL CONSTRUCTION

Model 1: Within Institution

The fully unconditional models provide evidence that dependent variables vary significantly across prisons and warrant the use of multilevel models (Table 3.2). Subsequent analysis addresses variation across prisons after the introduction of primary level-1 predictors and control variables (Model 1). These random-intercept models do not include level-2 variables. All continuous variables, including primary predictors and outcomes, are standardized to facilitate improved interpretation.

Primary investigation targets the impact of power and alienation on the primary outcomes and therefore control variables are fixed—slopes of these variables are not allowed to vary across prisons. Prior to full model construction, each primary predictor is modeled against each outcome variable and tested for slope variation across institutions. Hypotheses testing of fixed-versus random-slope models are employed to verify the improved status of the more complex model. In addition to verification of improved fit through hypothesis testing, the slopes of primary predictors are allowed to vary under the following conditions: significant variation across prisons ($p < 0.05$), reliability above 0.05, and tau correlations with other random predictors below 0.70. It is important to note that p-values that exceed 0.05 but are below 0.1 are also included but table footnotes denote actual p-value. The intercept is always set to vary randomly between prisons in order to facilitate the examination of group differences in means. All variables are centered on their grand mean (subtraction of overall mean from observed value). This provides more meaningful interpretation of coefficients and outcomes across years. Significance is noted by asterisk for p-values below 0.05. The HLM outputs record p-values for coefficients from two-tailed tests. Notably, hypotheses predict the direction of certain variables and therefore warrant one-tailed analysis for those variables. The p-Values between 0.05 and 0.10 are noted in the table footnote.

Model 2: Full Model

Initial level-2 analyses assess the relationship between prison-level controls and outcome variables (not shown). Geographical region remains in final models only if it is significant within the fully constructed model. Due to theoretical importance, variables pertaining to relational aspects of the institution (fear of inmates, perception of supervision, perception of peers through treatment orientation of facility) remain regardless of significance. Again, due to their central importance in the analysis, security levels also remain in the final models regardless of their significance. The full model includes level-2 and level-1 variables. When applicable (given the above conditions), level-1 primary predictors are permitted to vary. Subsequent models include cross-level interactions.

DESCRIPTIVE STATISTICS

Descriptive statistics for the key predictors and outcomes by year are listed in Table 3.1 (see also Tables 4.1 and 5.1). These constructed instruments have been standardized to allow for meaningful interpretation. The descriptive statistics represent the actual number of observations per variable. Due to missing data (a result of unanswered portions of the questionnaire) certain variables have fewer observations. To maximize observations per outcome, separate files were created to run analyses for each outcome.

Primary Outcome and Control Variables

Primary outcomes of interest are efficacy, emotional hardening, and institutional commitment. Efficacy is a self-report measure that averages 7-point Likert response to four survey questions (see Table 4.1). Answers range from "never" to "all the time." Prior research has not employed this measure to test power and alienation hypotheses. Emotional hardening is also a self-report measure that averages 7-point Likert responses to three survey questions (see Table 5.1). Answer categories range from "never" to "all the time." Institutional commitment is also a self-report measure that averages 7-point Likert responses to three survey questions (see Table 4.1). Answer categories range from "strongly disagree" to "strongly agree." Prior research has not used this measure to test power and alienation hypotheses. Chapters 4 and 5 detail the importance of these outcomes relevant to primary predictors (see Tables 4.1 and 5.1).

Race and gender are included in the level-1 predictions; but it is important to note that hypothesis testing indicates that race and gender effects do not vary consistently (and are neither consistently significant nor of central theoretical importance) across institutions and across years. These variables are fixed. I also propose that years of experience is preferable to age. Longer tenured officers are assumed to be more committed to the institution and to BOP practices as well as exhibit markedly different levels of alienation than their mid-tenured and new hire counterparts (Toch and Klofas 1982). Using the advice of Toch and Klofas (1982), I construct three dummy age variables: less than 5 years of experience; between 5 and 20 years experience; and over 20 years of experience. Since line-staff have direct contact with inmates (and are correctional officers) it is also critical to control for these workers. Lastly, I note the impact of less education (presumably less sophistication and less socialization) on key outcomes. (Weekly contact with inmates is also included as a binary variable in efficacy and hardening models.) The inclusion of the above demographics is warranted in that it provides for a cursory investigation into the salience of selection versus organization in predicting selected outcomes (e.g., Whitehead and Lindquist 1989).

Institutional Level Variables

Variables at the institutional level (level-2) allow for the analysis of the impact of aggregate measures on specific individual outcomes. Specific racial composition or general institutional sense of the quality of supervision (as examples) may impact individual perceived effectiveness of inmate supervision. In this regard, it is likely that environmental factors—aggregate measures as well as unique institutional identifiers (prison age, security level)—influence prison worker perception of power and of efficacy. Specific climate measures are critical components of prison ecosystem analysis.

Included variables at level-2 reflect theoretical arguments concerning alienation and power as well as empirical research regarding perception toward treatment or toward custody. Race Black appears to play a positive role in the individual perception of treatment and is therefore likely to have a greater impact on institutional perception of treatment when percentages of Race Black are higher. Race Black and gender are included in the model to control for the percentage of population that is female and percentage that is black by institution. (For clarity, it is proposed that larger female populations—as a percentage—may also impact commitment, efficacy, and hardening.)

Alienation is implicitly considered through the lens of environmental relationships. Relationships with charges, with peers, and with supervisors are important in this regard (Poole and Regoli 1981). To approximate these relationships, three specific measures are aggregated and included at level-2 (Table 3.2). Aggregate fear of inmates captures an overall institutional level measure of the relationship between prison workers and prisoners. Aggregate attitude toward supervisors captures the overall and general relationship between prison workers and their supervisors. Aggregate treatment orientation captures the general ideology of the individual prison—a factor best suited to measure the relationship promoted by prison workers within each institution and therefore an indicator of how that staff perceives the role of imprisonment at that institution. Aggregate treatment orientation might not necessarily be reflective of individual values but may reflect the assumed and thriving culture (Cullen et al. 1989; Toch and Klofas 1982). In addition, the aggregate level of commitment to treatment is warranted since treatment-oriented prisons may also differ in attitudes toward inmates (Jurik and Musheno 1986; Jackson and Ammen 1996). These three aggregate measures capture key relationships within the institution of confinement (see Poole and Regoli 1981) and are included as level-2 variables (Table 3.2). Although aggregate treatment orientation is specific to efficacy and alienation, it is included in commitment models as treatment orientation might impact power adoption, which may also impact one's commitment to the facility. These three specific factors are aggregations reported by workers within each institution sampled in the PSCS.

Additional environmental factors to consider for level-2 analysis include prison age, prison security level, and prison location. The age of the prison is controlled for on level-2 as a measure of the physical environment and "as a rough control for working conditions" (Camp, Saylor, and Harer 1997, 749). Security level is an appropriate proxy for the "dangerousness of inmates" housed in a specified institution (Camp, Saylor, and Harer 1997, 749). Security level progresses from low danger at a minimum-security facility to highest danger at a maximum-security prison. Prison location is included in the model in order to control for unobservable factors that pertain to geographical differences. Local conditions may impact commitment to particular institutions. It is admitted that this control is specific only to a general geographic area and does not account for proximity to urban centers or variation within specified geographical area.

Chapter 4

Power Adoptions
in Coercive Environments

Prisons are coercive institutions. In intended practice, chronic or severe violators of codified law are forcibly removed from the civil state and detained in secure facilities. These are state-sanctioned practices and, in essence, these practices reflect enforcement of collective morality. The prison institution, in this way, is an extension and symbol of the state's morality. Since coercion is central to the prison institution, I might infer that it is then illogical to demand prisoner acceptance of such an institution. To the external witness, prisons stand as icons of public order and of the public "good" and literally embody the power of the state: they physically confine men and women. But the external symbol and actual exercise of state power differ from the internal management of prison institutions. Incarceration may be legitimate to the public but it does not need to be legitimate to prisoners. I reason that the legitimacy of prison management diverges from the legitimacy of the prison institution. I would insist, therefore, that prison *management* should be perceived as procedurally fair to prisoners and to prison workers.

The central role of prison workers and prison administrators is to effectively manage and oversee safe and humane imprisonment practices. Therefore, the application of only coercive management techniques is probably misguided. Inside prisons, the manner in which power and authority are exercised may be integral to effective oversight: "prison work is all about the use of power and authority, deployed through human relationships. The stakes are high: the difference between good and bad practice can have life-threatening consequences" (Liebling 2011, 485). Admittedly, in order to induce conformity by prisoners, internal oversight may require legitimate power strategies. But there is a nontrivial distinction between prisons as legitimate institutions and prison managers as legitimate overseers. Tyler's (1990) conception of conforming behavior elevates the individual's perception of fairness. Per this argument, perceptions of fair treatment by the legal system increase the likelihood of conformity to societal rule and improve the individual's perception of the sanctioning body. Of course, this process is situational and perception is open to change through positive or negative experience (see also Sherman 1993). Notably, well-mannered sanctioning agents may improve behavior even if the sanction itself is unfavorable to the individual (see Paternoster et al. 1997). Acceptance is not necessarily required. I would find it inappropriate, thereby, to suppose that the prisoner should accept prison. I neither promote brutality nor advocate abolition. The prison itself is, and symbolizes, rigid authority. Although prison may be a necessary institution, the humanity that exists inside prison arguably exists in spite of—or in the face of—the prison (as a physical container not as a managed facility). The justification of forced confinement should not be confused with the prisoner's self-acceptance of that forced confinement. I believe the latter to be an unnatural acceptance and an illogical proposition.

Therefore, the real goal is not to legitimize the prison to the prisoner but to legitimize the prison to the prison worker. Much of the relational focus within prisons targets prisoner–staff relationships (Liebling 2004; Bottoms and Tankebe 2012). But I believe that the more important relationship in prison is between prison worker and prison administrator. I neither discount the prisoner nor presume his value as unimportant. In order to reach this conclusion on relationships, however, I take a somewhat circuitous (albeit short) route. The premise of legitimacy presumes that fair treatment will improve compliance and that unfair treatment will generate confrontation:

> every instance of brutality in prisons, every casual racist joke and demeaning remark, every ignored petition, every unwarranted bureaucratic delay, every inedible meal, every arbitrary decision to segregate or transfer without giving clear and well founded reasons, every petty miscarriage of justice, every futile and inactive period of time—is delegitimating. (Sparks and Bottoms 1995, 60)

The contention here is that brutality's impact on legitimacy is a central concern. This perspective places primacy on the prisoner–staff relationship and heavily weights prisoner perception. But brutal treatment violates the keeper philosophy and is counterproductive to population management. The inappropriate treatment listed by Sparks and Bottoms (1995) above would also be rejected by the keeper philosophy (DiIulio 1987). It simply is, in this regard, bad management. This type of oversight aggravates prisoners and makes imprisonment worse. But the above examples are only examples—they do not speak to the full range of injustice found within prison institutions and they do not begin to define injustice or generate a plausible management tool (outside of limiting the specific behavior listed above). The central concern,

thereby, actually becomes defining fair treatment—not legitimizing the institution. But what exactly is fair treatment and who defines it? Cross-cultural
definitions of fair treatment may reasonably vary. But in general, the conception of fair treatment appears to result from "right relationships." Fair treatment, presumably, reflects society's apparent moral consensus through these
relationships:

> Right relationships are those that do indeed respect the prisoner as a human
> being, take account of his welfare needs, and so on, yet at the same time uphold
> and maintain societal norms under which it was deemed necessary to require the
> individual to serve a prison sentence. Right relationships between prison staff
> and prisoners are therefore those that can be morally supported within the norms
> of society at large, and not simply demanded by those with a particular stake in
> the matter (in this instance, prisoners). (Bottoms and Tankebe 2012, 156)

It may be irrational to meet the whims of prisoners *and* it may be irrational
to brutalize prisoners. But prisoners do not define fair treatment and their
perception, therefore, should not be disproportionately weighted. My reading
of Bottoms and Tankebe (2012) is that if the demands of prisoners violate
the public's perception of fair treatment, then those demands are unreasonable (and not legitimized). The public, in this way, defines fair treatment and
through consensus makes the prison legitimate. Prisoners do not claim ter-
ritory outside of, or independent of, greater societal acceptance. Legitimacy
does not arrive by way of prisoner code or subculture. Per this logic, if behavior is morally rejected by society then it cannot be legitimized by prisons.
The perceived inherent contradiction of prison management appears to be
avoided. Prison stays are coerced but prison workers do not need to legitimize
that coercion. Legitimizing prison to the prisoner is, ultimately, improper.
Legitimacy of the institution is actually a reflection of societal norms.

I promote perceived legitimacy as central to prison work; but I also challenge its utility as an appropriate tool for prisoner management. As a member
of the public, the prison worker is encouraged to value the prison institution
as a legitimate place of punishment and therefore an appropriate state institution. But she does not need to *demand* that the prisoner accept that same
legitimacy. It is not the job of the prison worker to judge the prisoner or
justify his forced confinement and his guilt. Prison workers benefit from prisoners following the rules of prison but not necessarily accepting the prison
institution itself. I argued earlier that it is appropriate for prison workers to
assume that prisoners are indeed lawbreakers. But it is not appropriate for
those same workers to then attempt to legitimize the institution *to those prisoners*. Instead, prison workers should seek to ensure the safety and security
of all imprisoned and to champion the central tenet of the keeper philosophy:

loss of liberty is necessary and sufficient punishment. This is a challenging proposal. Ultimately, I ask for prison workers to withhold judgment but still maintain belief in the prison institution. The prison institution ideally stands as at least two bodies: one to the public (e.g., externally legitimate) and one to management (e.g., internally humane). Applying fair and consistent treatment as perceived by the prisoner may be very different than legitimizing the institution as perceived by the prisoner. I have argued that only the perception of the public is critical to institutional legitimacy in practice and in theory.

This discussion illustrates issues regarding the legitimacy of prison itself and not the employment of legitimate power strategies within prison. Drawing on legitimate power may still prove to be advantageous for prison management even if management is not attempting to legitimize the institution (and legitimate power is only one type of power available to prison managers). But it is important to emphasize that the discussion now moves away from prison itself to prison management itself. This is no longer strictly a question as to whether or not imprisonment itself can or should be justified (but, as will become apparent, this discussion cannot be set aside). This is a question of how prison workers perceive power and what impact that perception has on prisoner management. Presumably, power adoptions reflect internal processes. Prisons may be centrally about relationships (Liebling 2011) and those relationships may be subject to considerable variation. It is possible that management tactics differ within and across prison institutions. The control and the effectiveness of prisoner management may vary dramatically and may depend on the approach and the resources of the correctional officer. In practice, prison administrators are limited by the variety of power that they may employ. Power strategies are finite in number. To manage units, therefore, correctional officers must rely on one (or more than one) power strategy. Power adoptions shape the prison environment and they are the only tools that officers are able to employ. In a sense, all outcomes within the prison institution reflect a choice in power adoption. This is fundamental to the conceptualization of prison theory. If prisons are centrally about power, then power itself must dictate environment—both perceived and actual.

Hepburn (1985) illustrates five "bases of power" that influence the effectiveness of correctional management. My analysis largely draws on Hepburn's (1985) conceptualization. Depending on the adopted power strategy, the correctional officer may perceive and receive greater or less resistance to his command and this may impact his subsequent ability to maintain order during his tour. The central proposition is that prison workers adopt power strategies that are implicitly and explicitly promoted by prison hierarchy. Implicit power strategies may differ from institution to institution but are not randomly employed. Prison workers' perception of supervisor needs and requirements will largely dictate the perception of appropriate power deployment. Research has not examined the derivation of power adoption among federal prison workers. Notably, instead of defining power adoptions from the perspective of prisoners, this study endorses a position that asks prison workers to define power via their perception of the prison administration and their perception of supervision. In this regard, power arrives by way of management and therefore can be controlled or altered through directives. The central relationships, again, are within prison worker factions.

Essentially, I propose that institutions themselves promote power strategies and normative behavior arrives through active (or inactive) management and not through prisoners. As will become apparent, prison workers appear to gravitate toward inappropriate power exchanges in the absence of adequate administrative oversight. An unruly and violent housing unit is apparent to the entire institution; individual, isolated, and less severe infractions are far less visible and may go unnoticed and un-reprimanded in order to ensure that the housing unit goes unnoticed. There is incentive, in certain conditions, to overlook infractions.

In the following sections, I first review the available power strategies of prison institutions. Next I analyze the selected power adoptions by federal prison workers and the effect that those adopted power strategies have on prisoner management. It is important to note that I detail power adoptions within the general context of the prison environment—often understood from the perspective of the prisoner—and then apply these same premises to prison worker perception of appropriate power adoption through supervision and administration (empirical research has not yet evaluated prison worker perception of power as perceived through the prison hierarchy). The complexity of the prison environment necessarily requires multiple understandings of phenomena across populations. For even as an active prison administration may be responsible for dictating culture within housing units and the prison at large, an inactive or removed prison administration may be responsible for permitting the prisoners to dictate institutional culture (see Marquart and Roebuck 1985). Therefore, comprehension of power from multiple perspectives is germane to the overall discussion within the prison institution. But I still maintain that the central relationship of importance is between prison staff and prison managers.

LEGITIMATE POWER

The law, and the threat of punishment, may not be equally appreciated across individuals. Acute conformists and incorrigibles (see Pogarsky 2002) arguably are deterred or undeterred respectively without the risk of formal sanctions. Perspectives on and respect for moral authority—and the right thereof for that authority to discipline free citizens—could logically be based on positive or negative experiences with law enforcement illustrated by perceived bias or fairness of process and outcomes (see Tyler 1990). According to Tyler (1990), this perception of fairness influences the legitimacy individuals grant moral authorities such as law enforcement. It is likely that this perspective on fairness also permeates detention centers (see Tyler 2010).

Hepburn (1985, 146) contends: "legitimate power exists only to the extent that prisoners view the guards as having a legitimate right to give order *and be obeyed.*" But what power, given that the correctional officer is a variety of moral authority (as an agent of the state financed to properly supervise inmate populations), do prisoners bestow upon their guardians? The comparison between police and correctional officers as moral authorities here begins to split. Portions of the general population are acute conformists—unwilling to stray from lawful behavior perhaps due to strict socialization. The natural conditions of policing permit exposure to citizens with favorable orientations toward the police. The natural work environment of correctional officers consists of populations who have refused to conform (in one manner or another). These populations are less likely to defer to the demands of this "moral" authority (Hepburn 1985). Importantly, legitimacy in terms of prison populations also differs from legal cynicism within free populations. Prisons detain men and women who have violated codified law—the state holds them against their will. Legal cynicism prevents free populations from utilizing state resources to solve and prevent local crime problems. This cynical citizen chooses *not* to involve police or the courts. Relative to the state guardian (or the correctional institution), the prisoner does not have the same type of choice. His life is dictated by formal control.

But it does not automatically follow, even given these environmental differences, that legitimacy cannot be obtained and maintained in the prison setting. Fair and consistent application of sanctions—administered with respect and with objective reason (deserved, substantively just)—should increase conformity. Generally this proposition would promote correctional officer legitimacy through a "fairness proxy" such as just infraction application. Correctional officers who appeared to support fairness and consistency in the application of infractions would garner greater respect, and therefore greater *legitimate* power, from the prisoner population. Indeed, institutional analysis suggests that negative perceptions of infraction enforcement do appear to be related to increased violence (see Bierie 2013). Reflecting defiance theory (Sherman 1993), perception of this fairness is central: it is not only the sanctioning but also the perception of the sanctioning that causes the prisoner to perceive a body to be legitimate. Selective infraction application does not necessarily minimize this legitimacy, if consistently applied across diverse populations.

Somewhat ironically, however, comprehensive infraction application is likely to harbor resentment among prisoners, which may indeed increase grievances. Indeed, a strict emphasis on rule adherence has complex consequences. For the prisoner, selective sanctioning may increase legitimate power. For the officer, selective sanctioning may be necessary when legitimate power, or institutional support, is limited. I concede that complete rule enforcement may be impossible, ineffective, and unpopular with prisoners and for prison administrators (Sykes 1956); "If guards attempt to enforce all the rules, they risk being evaluated as rigid or punitive. Conversely, if they are discovered exercising undue discretion or overlooking infractions, they risk being accused of incompetence or corruption" (Poole and Regoli 1980b, 217). But without complete rule enforcement, formal rules are replaced, at least in part, by informal rules. This may not concern the prisoner. Regardless of the formality or informality of the enforcement, she desires consistent and unbiased treatment. But for the prison administrator, legitimate power is reflective of official edict. Adopting informal strategies reduces effective oversight and undermines the official intention of prison (and the overall impact of prison managers). This is a dilemma.

But perceived treatment is not static. Legitimacy is an ongoing exchange: "legitimacy is not a fixed phenomenon but constitutes 'a perpetual discussion,' a continuing dialogue between those who hold power and the recipients" (Liebling 2011, 486; see also Bottoms and Tankebe 2012). This is generally understood as action between prisoners and prison staff. But prisoners ("recipients") neither *choose* prison nor *choose* their captors. Even internal chaos would not alter this fundamental reality. Prisoners remain in prison because they are detained, coerced. I do not discount the potential value of exchange and dialogue between prison staff and prisoners. The prison environment is somewhat fluid in that the needs of prisoners vary and fluctuate. But prisoners are not able to challenge the pecking order of the institution. And, as I have explained above, there is a subtle but important distinction between the legitimacy of the prison institution itself and the employment of legitimate power within the prison institution. Treatment within facility can be deemed fair even if the institution is not. In essence, dialogue may be advantageous in order to find mutual footing between prisoners and prison workers. But that footing—at least theoretically—reflects the greater collective morality of society (see Bottoms and Tankebe 2012; Bottoms and Sparks 1995). Dialogue does not promote equal exchange. The rules do not come from the prisoners. Legitimate power comes from prison management. Certainly, perceived fair treatment is integral to effective management. But for the prison worker perceived fair treatment may be complicated due to active and assertive competing factions. Understanding and enforcing a collective morality is challenging.

I have reasoned that the relationship *among* prison workers is instrumental to effective prison management. Treatment by supervisors—as perceived by the prison worker—reinforces or undermines the legitimate authority of the prison. To maintain and promote legitimate power among prison staff, the process is nuanced. Prison managers must achieve two goals: legitimize prison itself and legitimize their own authority. Legitimate power is rooted in the just authority of the prison institution *and* the perceived fair treatment by that institution. Generally, prison administrators can legitimize the prison institution for its workers by consistently treating them fairly and proving that the prison itself is an appropriate place for punishment (the perceived treatment of prisoners by staff may inevitably taint this picture but only insofar as that treatment appears irrational and unfair). Since perception is integral, constant dialogue and exchange (e.g., explanation and justification for behavior) are necessary for the continual employment of legitimate power by prison staff. In practice, the employment of legitimate power follows rules of official conduct—behavior recognized and endorsed by the administrators as fair treatment. Legitimate power promotes humane tactics. The prison worker presumably adopts legitimate power strategies in the first place because she subscribes to institutional ethos (since the institution and prison managers treat her fairly). In turn, lack of prison brutality then increases the public's perception of prison legitimacy and of prison work.

Management matters. Prison workers must possess both the ability to apply fair treatment and the good sense and socialization to subscribe to the prison institution itself. Empowering the prison worker is key to this success. If legitimate power is culturally reinforced, then belief in the legitimacy of the institution should increase the perceived ability to manage prisoners. Official oversight defined by supervision and training should also increase the perceived effectiveness of prisoner management. The ability to manage, in this instance, is derived from official, or *legitimate*, sources. Those prison workers who employ legitimate power derive their sense of power from official channels—supervisors, core values, and institutional procedures. This insight is critical. If the power strategy arrives by way of official channels then it is productive and legitimate. This is not overly problematic in that the BOP does not officially sanction inhumane or abusive treatment of prisoners.

Measuring Legitimacy

Commitment to the BOP is used as one proxy for legitimate power. The BOP officially sanctions humane treatment of inmates. Commitment to the BOP suggests a commitment to this philosophy and a commitment to official standards of treatment. Commitment to the Bureau of Prisons does differ from institutional commitment. Hence, this measure implies that the prison worker subscribes to the BOP in general—to its philosophy, to its practices, and (implicitly) to its *right* to incarcerate. I contend, at least in this instance, that it is an unlikely and indeed illogical proposition that an individual ascribes fidelity to an institution or an organization whose sole purpose and reason for being she fundamentally rejects. An additional way to conceive of legitimacy is via fairness. Since one purpose of this inquiry is to ascertain prison workers' perceptions of power through their institution of employment, the perception of fairness will increase the sense of legitimacy in the system and in the prison itself (Sherman 1993). Both of these measures are constructed through survey data in federal prisons. Principal component factor analysis confirms that the selected variables do in fact sufficiently load onto a single factor for each constructed measure (Table 4.1).

COERCIVE POWER

Unjust employment of power could understandably result in negative detainee response. The *right* to employ power does differ from the simple *ability* to employ power. Although ostensibly similar, coercive and legitimate powers diverge in that "coercive power is based on the prisoners' perception that guards have the ability to punish disobedience" (Hepburn 1985, 147). Coercive power is not limited to the perception of unjust application. Presumably, a correctional officer concerned by legitimate power would invest more in the just authority of his actions whereby that same officer consumed by coercive authority would merely entertain the possibility of applying punishment on the detained population. This distinction is important in that responses to these two varying types of power application could be dramatically different. In line with Sherman (1993), perceived unfair sanctions result in *defiance*—a behavioral response that refuses to acknowledge the authority of the sanctioning agent. The prison environment—with continual searches, punitive segregation units, and access to physical and even lethal force—lends itself to the possibility of compromise and abuse of power. The mere ability to search cells does not warrant the search—especially from the perspective of the inmate (but arguably, from the perspective of most trained correctional officers as well).

Coercive power appears to offer little reward to prison managers—and instead may only increase the likelihood of revolt or deviance (Hepburn 1985, 147). Beyond its opposition to the "keeper philosophy," it is not clear that common misuse of power serves a real purpose in prisons since "many prisoners feel that the punishments which can be imposed on a daily basis

Table 4.1   Specified Construction of Dependent and Power Measures (*Alpha scores for 2007, 2008, 2009, 2010; Factor loading for correlation with latent variable, 2007*)

	Alpha Scores (2007, 2008, 2009, 2010)	Factor Loading (Year 2007)
Institutional Commitment	0.8221, 0.8224, 0.8036, 0.8139	
This facility is the best in the whole BOP		0.8099
I would rather be stationed at this facility than any other I know about		0.8974
I would like to continue to work at this facility		0.8730
Efficacy	0.7400, 0.7451, 0.7434, 0.7327	
An ability to deal very effectively with the problems of inmates		0.6859
A feeling that you are positively influencing other people's lives through your work		0.8493
A feeling of accomplishment after working closely with inmates		0.8227
A feeling that you can easily create a relaxed atmosphere with inmates		0.6321
Legitimate Power 1	0.8971, 0.9081, 0.9065, 0.9050	
I have a good opinion of the BOP most of the time		0.8838
Most of the time BOP is run very well		0.8785
I am usually satisfied with the BOP		0.8982
The BOP is better than any of the other correctional agencies (e.g., State)		0.7903
If I remain in corrections, I would prefer to remain with the BOP		0.7530
Legitimate Power 2	0.8168, 0.8336, 0.8115, 0.8262	
Standards used to evaluate me are fair		0.8844
Performance rating was fair		0.8456
Supervisor gives feedback for good work		0.8382
Coercive Power		
Supervisor intimidates me		
Reward Power		
I will get a cash award or unscheduled pay increase if I perform especially well		

Table 4.1   (cont.)

Expert Power	0.7536, 0.7643, 0.7402, 0.7324	
The BOP training program does not prepare me or help me deal with situations that arise on the job*		0.7280
Training at this facility has improved my job skills		0.8474
My BOP training has helped me to work effectively with inmates		0.8867
Referent Power	0.8330, 0.8394, 0.8715, 0.8671	
Boss encourages my ideas about job		0.8735
Boss asks my opinion about work problems		0.8879

Source: Data from the PSCS, Federal Bureau of Prisons, 2007–2010.
All constructed measures load sufficiently onto a single factor for every year (2007 shown). Each response scaled seven points from "strongly disagree" to "strongly agree".
*Reverse Coded.

do not materially differ from the level of punishment they endure by being incarcerated" (Hepburn 1985, 147). Coercion, in this subtler form, would not increase compliance. With suitable prison oversight, rampant and excessive abuses of power should be minimized and therefore coercive power would be relegated to minor instances (Marquart 1986; DiIulio 1987)—which, it is argued here, would not increase compliance. This is not to suggest that physical torture or excessive deprivation (instances that are not formally permitted) would not be effective at increasing compliance—however inhumane they may be. It could be argued that coercive power is merely the officer voicing her ability to punish—not necessarily an acknowledgement of abuse. This assertion would suggest that the officer is able to "penalize those who do not cooperate" (Hepburn 1985, 151). The variation applied here implies the mere *ability*—which may or may not be in line with authority and objective fairness.

At its logical extreme, coercive power implies (mis)use of force. And there is empirical support for the idea of inappropriate use of force in prison settings. In the mid-1980s in Texas, Marquart (1986, 348) observes: "Guards' use of force was a socially structured tactic of prisoner control that was well entrenched in the guard culture." Subculture development and value transmission of appropriate coercive behavioral responses was key to what could most aptly be described as misuse of power (guards systematically and overzealously employed physical violence against inmates). Marquart (1986) highlights the lack of a strong central authority and proper administrative oversight as complacent in the development and continued existence of such informal control mechanisms (see also DiIulio 1987). Coercion in this environment benefited the correctional officer individually in that it aided in promotions (as it reflected "culturally positive" qualities in the officer) and collectively in that it garnered officer "solidarity" and maintained order within the prison (Marquart 1986). The use of force, although encouraged, was strictly managed, apparently in an effort to evade formal detection and official rebuke. This behavior was encouraged by a set of proscriptions and prescriptions. By unofficial code, for example, officers were not to engage in physical violence in the presence of multiple witnesses, such as in the dining hall. These latter observations are of particular interest in this study in that they reflect the possibility of culturally prescribed normative behaviors within correctional settings. Prison workers derive coercive power strategies from coworkers, especially supervisors. Coercive power is based simply on the ability to punish.

The BOP has had a strong central authority since its founding in the 1930s. Prior to 1930, federal prisons did suffer from abuse and scandal without such oversight (DiIulio 1991a). As Marquart (1986, 362) notes: "prison organizations based on centralization and formalization (with little autonomy and discretion), such as the California system or the Federal Bureau of Prisons, will not support an inmate control system predicated on coercion and fear." Chronic employment of coercive force in federal prisons is highly unlikely. But mistrust of superiors by officers could create a more complex environment in which the line-staff perceive the administration to be unfairly and erratically meting out punishment of staff: the correctional officer "resents may of the actions of his superiors—the reprimands, the lack of ready appreciation, the incomprehensible order—and in the inmates he finds willing sympathizers: they too claim to suffer from the unreasonable caprice of power" (Sykes 1956, 260). This scenario creates an environment in which coercive power from administration creates solidarity between inmates and line-staff.

Measuring Coercion

Supervisors that intimidate staff members draw on coercive power strategies (see Table 4.1). Intimidation reflects the mere ability to employ power rather than the appropriate employment of that power. By definition intimidating characteristics are not legitimate. I propose that this power variety yields low commitment to the institution and increases hardening of prison workers.

REWARD POWER

Consistent with the learning perspective that positive reinforcement of behavior X will increase incidence of behavior X (see Akers 1977), reward power implicitly adopts the perspective that correctional officers must engage in exchange for effective supervision. Appropriately, "this power base is sustained by the creation of a system of informal rewards" (Hepburn 1985, 147). Although often cloaked in an altruistic disguise, reward power is little more than quid pro quo. The correctional officer understands the burden of oversight—potentially greatly outnumbered—and is likely without administrative support. The officer's drive toward bargaining, as it were, may be driven by benevolent intentions—but likely devolves into a prisoner hierarchy whereby select inmates are given preferential treatment, perhaps even allowed supervision of other inmates (see Cloward 1968; Marquart and Roebuck 1985). This transfer of power has met with unquestionably brutal outcomes in the past (Useem and Kimball 1989). Prisons are not intended to be democracies nor are inmates proven to be willing to accept entrance into mutual behavioral contracts while incarcerated.

While it is conceded that reward power may provide correctional officers with needed informal rewards to encourage behavioral sanity, especially on housing units, it is not clear how this type of power would increase the authority of the prison administration and improve the overall order of not just the prison but the effectiveness of other correctional officers who must also monitor the housing units and the halls and whose perspectives toward bargaining may not only differ from their colleagues but may also place them in danger due to their potential divergence. But this may be an inaccurate inference. Reward power may be a consequence of organizational inadequacy. Hepburn (1985, 147) insists, "deficiencies of legitimate power, coercive power, and formal rewards compel guards to establish an informal norm of reciprocity with prisoners by which resources are exchanged." Reward power may emerge due to extant conditions, rather than create those conditions. Increasing legitimate power may undermine the necessity of such an informal and unregulated version of power. But in order to increase line-staff legitimacy, prison administrations may need to specifically reinforce and laud officer performance. Even selective (or rare) use of infractions is undermined if officially labeled as excessive or met without formal punitive response. Prison administrators, consequently, increase line-staff legitimacy and perceived discretion by honoring and upholding inmate infractions (without clear evidence of bias or corruption). Upholding written infractions in prison court signifies management's support of the officer. This is only one example in which prison administrators can improve legitimate power. Trust in administrators, in turn, may be a key indicator in adoption of legitimate power techniques. Consequently, mistrust in prison administrators or in direct supervisors may indicate the need to employ informal methods of population management.

Perhaps the more relevant point is that without official support officers may be amenable to inappropriate exchange with inmates, but this exchange is largely insignificant. Hepburn (1985) defines reward power as: "I can give special help and benefits to those who cooperate with me" (151). As such, the adequate definition of reward power may simply be the likelihood that correctional officers will attempt to curry favor among the detained population in order to increase the boredom of their tours (a positive outcome). It does not appear that devolving into an inmate hierarchy is a prerequisite for utilization of reward power. Instead, as individuals continually operate in exchange so may correctional officers engage in common—even simple—exchanges during their tours. This exchange could be as simple as trading kitchen cleanup for longer hours in the day room—an exchange that does not provide the inmate recipient with peer supervision or undue guardianship over other, potentially vulnerable, populations. Taking reward power to its logical extremes draws a horrific illustration, reflective of "building-tenders" and "turn-keys" (Marquart and Roebuck 1985). But for daily operations, and on an extremely small scale, reward power may be necessary, instrumental, and harmless.

This does not address the issue of prison worker perception of reward power and the derivation of this perception. For the prison worker, reward power is reflective of special treatment due to performance. From this perspective, improved job performance yields favorable placements and pay increases. Compliance with formal institutional procedures and individual instruction improves the likelihood of reaping benefits from an informal reward system (i.e., not specifically outlined in bureau or institutional policy). Subscription to this tenet partly undermines the legitimacy understood in bureau and institutional commitment since that commitment is a product of informal and inappropriately perceived exchange.

Measuring Reward Power

In prison environments, reward power is generally defined as an informal and reciprocal relationship with prisoners that permits and promotes the exchange of services. Hepburn (1985) considers reward power to be: "I can give special help and benefits to those who cooperate with me." In this context, prison workers believe that if they perform well they will get special rewards. Again, the present focus argues that power derivations often arrive through institutional channels (see Table 4.1). Here, the prison worker subscribes to the notion that "unofficial" assistance will curry favor with his supervisors and will result in monetary rewards. This subscription would largely be supported only in an environment that, in practice, supported such activity.

EXPERT POWER

Given the confrontational nature of the prison environment—specifically, the reasons for and consequences of forced confinement—correctional officers may find it difficult to garner respect from prisoners due to special knowledge or advanced skill. As Hepburn (1985, 148) writes: "prisoners are loathe to acknowledge competence among guards." The utility of expert power is probably best demonstrated in the relationship between medical doctor and patient—a relationship that depends dearly on the acute awareness and perceptibility of a reasonably trained professional. It is not clear that correctional officers provide services in high demand. Medical doctors assess patient viability and recommend treatments that reflect the best possibility for the organism to thrive and survive. The utility of expert power for the correctional officer appears to pale in respect to the other bases of power, especially legitimate power. The trust the patient places in the medical doctor is trust in diagnosis based in years of training. The trust the prisoner potentially places in the correctional officer is trust in fairness and consistency (a precarious and easily undone trust, of course). The value of specialized skill from a management perspective—beyond the ability to maintain order and supervise adequately (critical components to a highly professional occupation)—arguably counters the mission of custody and control. Hepburn (1985, 148–149) admits that, "expert power is undermined by bureaucratic administrative procedures." Uniformity and predictability trump correctional officer's independence. These observations do not preclude the possibility that expert power permeates detention centers but rather question how useful this expertise is to the overall goal of prison administration and order maintenance.

Expert power requires that "prisoners perceive that guards have some special skill, knowledge, or expertise" (Hepburn 1985, 148). Special skill and knowledge reflect the ability to improve the conditions of the mental and physical world of the detained population. Nuanced comprehension of the institution (and of correctional practices) and the ability to navigate that institution reflects the specific utility of expert power. If power is something that may be employed then one may assert that expert power is beneficial in navigating the conflicting goals of treatment and custody. Experience may actually increase the ease of solving inmate grievances or concerns. Thorough knowledge of the work, in short, makes for a more effective worker. Power, here, derives from expertise in the workings of the prison—not expertise in psychotherapy, drug addiction, or counseling. But does the correctional officer actually acquire special skills that elevate him to a truly unique provider of care? Liebling (2011, 488) asserts that the prison worker does in fact acquire skills that make him unique:

So, what is distinctive about prison officer work is that it is based on, or requires, a sophisticated, dynamic and often subtle use of power, through enduring and challenging relationships, which has effects on the recipients. This is highly skilled work. Competence in this area—in the use of authority—contributes most to prisoner perceptions of the quality of life in, or moral performance of, a prison.

Liebling's observation is intriguing. And, with her assistance, I reason that expert power may actually be the advanced ability to effectively employ *other* types of power. Indeed, Hepburn's (1985) definition of expert power may be incomplete. Hepburn defines expert power as: "I have the competence and good judgment about things to know what is best" (Hepburn 1985, 151). This does not directly address experience or reflect Liebling's (2011) insistence that prison work is "highly skilled work." And mere ability to resolve conflicts runs awkwardly close to coercive and legitimate power bases. Admittedly, Hepburn (1985, 148) does draw on the importance of advanced skill: "guards are likely to believe that their expertise in resolving conflicts and determining the appropriate course of prisoner behavior warrants the compliance of prisoners." The prisoner perception of expert power emphasizes the unique and realized ability of the prison worker due to circumstances beyond status. But a more appropriate perspective may propose that prison workers perceive greater effectiveness in population management through increased emphasis in training and skill obtainment. In this way, expert power may be a tool that can then adequately exercise other forms of power. I find this perspective preferable to an ambiguous definition that sees expert power as an unclear variant of experience.

But the specific utility of expert power is still unclear. Prison organizations demand uniformity in administering punishment and oversight and this uniformity potentially zaps the independence of the individual correctional officer in making decisions outside procedural norms. This conclusion would be dramatically undermined if correctional officer rulebooks specifically failed to comment on correct procedure following common and even uncommon detention center occurrences (since expert power suggests autonomy in decision making for each officer). Otherwise, the statement—"I have the competence and good judgment about things to know what is best"—merely suggests that the officer is able to follow the rules. But irrespective of actual autonomy constraints, prison workers' *perception* of expertise—as manifested through discretion— may still empower and directly impact perception of prisoner management. Prison workers who believe they are able to shape events presumably also believe that (1) they have greater expertise and (2) they are more effective at their jobs. The tool of expert power then is valuable but largely perceptual.

Notably, discretion and role definitions may have changed throughout the mid- to late-20th century. Lombardo (1989) found that correctional officer philosophy and practice in the 1970s promoted, to a certain degree, a "helper" mentality that created a series of potentially concerning realities. This environmental posture ostensibly prevented the escalation of minor issues and may have increased the civility of the workplace (see Lombardo 1989, 80) but may also have damaged the effectiveness of overall administrative control and legitimacy. Heading off potential problem escalation (and interceding adequately) required offering "free" advice or obtaining intimate knowledge of inmate lives. But effective intervention due to the correctional officer's intimate knowledge of inmate emotion and predicament often results in the precarious development of solidarity between officer and inmate (see Lombardo 1989, 86). Perceived inadequacy of the bureaucratic administration—by both officer and inmate—likely engenders this arrangement. While the 1980s appeared to witness a turn toward procedural and directive adherence (reflective of the earlier propositions regarding expert power), Lombardo's (1989) illustration of the 1970s draws *expert* power as emblematic of personal and intimate knowledge of inmate discourse and activity, often at the expense of the hierarchy. In this instance, expert power derived its strength by individual mandate rather than organizational or role mandate. The medical doctor derives her expert power by way of medicine—objective comprehension of anatomy; the correctional officer appears to derive expert power by living in a shared environment: "the walls of the prison emphasize divisions between guards and inmates while they also draw the two groups together as people sharing a common environment" (Lombardo 1989, 86). Undeniably, these are human environments with individuals as captors and captives. This daily interaction may harmlessly benefit the inmate in that seasoned correctional officers understand the inner workings of the prison; this daily interaction may also harm the effectiveness of order maintenance and directives in that inmate dilemmas are not handled consistently across units and across staff.

Measuring Expert Power

Expert power is largely derived from the effectiveness of training as it applies to correctional work. An increase in the prison worker's perception that training has improved her ability to manage inmates will subsequently increase her sense of expert power. Reflective of special knowledge or advanced skill, expert power arrives through institutional provision and improves the prison worker's perception of her employment abilities.

REFERENT POWER

The most ambiguous of the power bases is referent power. Hepburn (1985, 149) contends: "a guard will have power over prisoners to the extent that prisoners respect and admire the guard." Ostensibly, this perspective highlights the importance of fair treatment and consistency—clear emblems of legitimate power. But the notion of *respect* is deeply embedded in criminological literature, specifically in reference to urban, alienated populations (see Anderson 1999). In harmlessly defining *referent* power in the following statement—"Because of the way I get along with inmates, they want to do what will get my respect and admiration" (Hepburn 1985, 151)—Hepburn potentially overlooks the self-governing and aggressive connotation attached to this ideal. As he insists: "Guards who are fair and evenhanded in their relations with prisoners, who display a degree of respect to the prisoners, who fulfill their promises to prisoners, and who exercise their coercive power with impartiality and without malice gain respect among prisoners" (Hepburn 1985, 149). If this is the condition under which respect is gained, then this type of power would be better understood as a variant of legitimate power—fairness and consistency create a level of respect for the correctional institution and the correctional officer. Among populations that may harbor a deep mistrust of formal authority—perhaps due to perceived biases by formal agents of the criminal justice system—gaining respect may be either a foolhardy goal or a sign of abuse and mismanagement. This is not a debate regarding the value of respect. Instead, this notes the potential convergence of the intended meaning of *referent* with the actual meaning of *legitimate*. These two terms merge in practice and in self-report. Respecting correctional officers—as intended by referent power—is actually a variant of legitimate power. Referent power, as *unintended* by Hepburn (1985), is still a critical area of interest as it potentially uncovers divergence toward acquiescence to prisoner normative behavior. This variant of *referent* power would most likely be linked to a darker side of *reward* power.

Referent power may also have blossomed, in earlier decades, due to the intentional attempt on behalf of the correctional officer to reduce the likelihood that minor inmate issues became major inmate issues (see Lombardo 1989). Some officers in Auburn Prison in the 1970s went so far as to "*take affirmative steps to discover* if particular inmates in particular circumstances are having difficulties. This strategy requires the officer not only to be reactive, but to be the initiator of interactions involving 'human services' intervention" (Lombardo 1989, 82, italics in original). While concerns for protocol and even possible manipulation trumped many human service intercessions in the 1980s, during the 1970s, correctional officers who willfully aided inmates with personal or logistical dilemmas may have gained greater respect and greater referent power: "when helping inmates with problems, guards do so in face of perceived peer and administrative condemnation. Not being *paid* to counsel makes guard assistance real" (Lombardo 1989, 86, italics in original). But even in this 1970s, the accruement of referent power still appeared to be at the cost of the overall prison authority. Inmates perceived the correctional officer as operating outside of his duties—against the order of the prison—and therefore respected his counsel. This may be as simple as respecting the counsel as arriving by way of an individual, another human actor (as opposed to by way of an official institutional perspective), but it is undeniable that this respect is connected to, and arrives by way of, a sort of rebellion on behalf of the correctional officer.

Unlike the above nascence of referent power through confrontation and mild rebellion, institutional employment of referential power engenders empowerment and unity. Empowerment increases the likelihood that prison workers will perceive their work and their own usefulness as integral to the success of the institution. From this perspective, referent power could most aptly be defined as the respect prison workers feel that they receive from their supervisors. The effective use of referent power by prison management may improve prison worker morale. Prison workers that perceive systematic and individual encouragement and respect will perform more professionally and more effectively. Notably, institutions have the ability to control the level of applied referent power by way of adequate supervision.

Measuring Referent Power

Generally, referent power in prison environments is reflective of the extent that prisoners respect and admire the guard or prison officer. In the context of this analysis, however, referent power refers to the respect prison workers feel that they receive from supervisors and from their work in general. An increase in the sense that ideas are respected will result in greater ability to manage inmate populations and will increase commitment to the institution (Table 4.1).

INSTITUTIONAL POWER ADOPTION
AND EFFICACY IN PRISONER OVERSIGHT

I submit that institutional commitment is an appropriate proxy for what types of power are employed within specific institutional settings. Institutional commitment captures unique attachment to the direct institution of employment (see Table 4.1). Regardless of the centralization of authority, numerous environmental factors may either diminish or increase the commitment to a particular institution, irrespective of the individual's commitment to the BOP. For example, if coercive and reward power increase institutional commitment then this suggests that the institution promotes, presumably informally, coercion and mistrust. This also suggests that institutions largely promote an organizational milieu that is understood across the facility and that practices within the facility are understood and endorsed on an informal and formal level. It does not require informal practices that counter formal decree—but it does open up the possibility that a specific institution harbors unique types of individuals and may approach management in a divergent manner due to the specifics of the institution. Regardless, commitment to a specific institution should reflect an appreciation, and an acceptance, of that particular institution's cultural normative code (which might vary from the overall governing body's aim). Since institutional commitment varies significantly across institutions, it is further likely that different types of facilities—different in terms of security, location, supervision, and prisoner and worker composition—operate in divergent fashion and do not capture prison worker acceptance uniformly. This is hardly surprising. By definition, a maximum-security prison requires a different set of protocol than a minimum-security prison. The experiences, thereby, will be different.

I also generate a measure that captures the individual prison worker's perceived efficacy of inmate management. This measure was initially designed by Saylor (1984). I reconstruct this measure, using Saylor's operationalization, through principal components factor analysis (Table 4.1). This measure implies that effectiveness in inmate management also includes personal accomplishment. The work brings rewards. Otherwise it could be argued that the prison worker is ineffective at working with prisoners since it brings no feelings of accomplishment or positive influence (i.e., his work has not improved his condition). It is important to note that the efficacy measure reflects satisfaction with current employment through inmate contact *or* through contact with other workers. Surveys are self-reports of perceptions and not necessarily objective measures. Effectiveness in working with prisoners is bolstered by attention to overall perception of the importance of the work in general. Prisoner management entails more than prisoner interaction. Perception of a positive influence on others reflects belief in effectiveness. It is important to include a measure, therefore, that captures this nuance. I admit that it is not possible to construct an objective measure of efficacy. Perceptual measures will all suffer from the same inadequacies. It cannot be overstated, however, that the role of the prison worker is to oversee prisoners.

PRISON POWER ADOPTION

In order to ascertain the type of power strategy adopted by federal institutions, I generated power variables (Table 4.1) and predicted institutional commitment as a framework to guide analysis.

Hypothesis 1a: *Legitimate, referent, and expert power improve institutional commitment for the prison worker. Coercive and reward power reduce institutional commitment.*

I first contend that legitimate, referent, and expert power positively and significantly predict institutional commitment. Legitimate power reflects formal management strategy and an individual's overall subscription to the will of the governing body. Belief in the *right* for a prison institution to incarcerate and belief that the BOP is an adequate and reasonable governing body is inherent in its ability to exercise legitimate power. In this regard, heightened commitment in this area implies that the BOP can successfully act on its will since the worker subscribes positively to it as an employer. Expert power implies that the worker perceives that he has received sufficient training to meet the demands of prison work. The ability to handle the demands of prison work does not necessary arise from specific training regimes. This variety of power specifically identifies the source of skill obtained by way of developed training programs through the Bureau of Prisons. Expert power also reflects the formal provisions granted to the worker. Referent power highlights the value of respect and the role that professional and appropriate supervision can play in the prison management. These three power strategies should increase local commitment—or commitment to the specific institution of employment.

My analysis indicates that Hypothesis (1a) is supported and holds across years of analysis (Table 4.2). This consistent and robust finding suggests that federal institutions implicitly promote formal and constructive types of power within their facilities. Official power strategies are reflected in mission statements. Unofficially adopted power strategies are by definition informal expressions. By selecting institutional commitment as a suitable proxy for the individual institution's power adoption, it is possible to uncover these informal expressions of power. This outcome is also able to provide insight into what improves morale. Results indicate that prison workers are more committed to institutions that they believe are legitimate and that provide them with adequate training to fulfill job requirements. Prison workers are also more committed to institutions that respect them. Said differently, federal institutions appear to adopt power strategies that empower workers through respect, training, and transparency. It is important to note that the power strategies

Table 4.2   Institutional Commitment Regressed on Power Adoptions (*HLM with REML and robust standard errors*)

	Model 2 2007	Model 2 2008	Model 2 2009	Model 2 2010
	Coefficient (Stand. Error)	Coefficient (Stand. Error)	Coefficient (Stand. Error)	Coefficient (Stand. Error)
Institutional Level				
Intercept	−0.012	−0.006	0.052*	0.007
	(0.021)	(0.022)	(0.025)	(0.025)
Supervision	−0.010	0.108	0.039	−0.000
	(0.072)	(0.081)	(0.077)	(0.086)
Orientation	0.143	−0.082	−0.021	0.056
	(0.088)	(0.091)	(0.106)	(0.143)
Fear	−0.260***	−0.115*	−0.153*	−0.149*
	(0.038)	(0.045)	(0.062)	(0.062)
Prison Age	0.004***	0.003***	0.001*	0.002**
	(0.000)	(0.000)	(0.000)	(0.000)
Gender	−0.523	−0.044	−0.210	−0.037
	(0.288)	(0.298)	(0.254)	(0.372)
Race	−0.413**	−0.446**	−0.436**	−0.511**
	(0.136)	(0.134)	(0.131)	(0.169)
High Security	−0.125	−0.137	−0.098	−0.043
	(0.096)	(0.104)	(0.120)	(0.137)
Medium Security	−0.075	0.004	−0.099	−0.079
	(0.061)	(0.064)	(0.080)	(0.081)
Low Security	−0.228***	−0.064	−0.189*	−0.131
	(0.058)	(0.063)	(0.079)	(0.093)
Individual Level				
Legitimate Power	0.436***	0.442***	0.426***	0.434***
	(0.020)	(0.020)	(0.024)	(0.018)
Coercive Power	−0.022	−0.025*	−0.010	−0.003
	(0.015)	(0.013)	(0.019)	(0.013)
Reward Power	0.023	0.028	0.003	0.041**
	(0.014)	(0.016)	(0.018)	(0.014)
Expert Power	0.093***	0.102***	0.072**	0.063***
	(0.016)	(0.017)	(0.021)	(0.015)
Referent Power	0.086***	0.111***	0.134***	0.108***
	(0.017)	(0.016)	(0.024)	(0.016)
Race Black	−0.034	−0.095*	−0.021	−0.098*
	(0.043)	(0.038)	(0.050)	(0.037)
Female	0.011	0.017	−0.014	−0.028
	(0.027)	(0.025)	(0.037)	(0.026)
20+ Years at BOP	0.129**	−0.013	0.056	0.004
	(0.043)	(0.036)	(0.044)	(0.038)
College	−0.038	−0.079**	−0.042	−0.036
	(0.027)	(0.025)	(0.037)	(0.023)
Line-Staff	0.052	0.115***	0.134***	0.172***
	(0.029)	(0.028)	(0.034)	(0.031)
Variance Components	X^2	X^2	X^2	X^2
U_0	323.930***	351.342***	312.291***	531.534***
$U_{Legitimate}$	182.977***	145.659*	166.391**	180.949***
$U_{Referent}$	146.382*	140.254	157.175**	—

Source: Data from the PSCS, Federal Bureau of Prisons, 2006–2010.
*p<0.05; **p<0.01; ***p<0.001.

that improve commitment are also important to adopt in order to improve communication and morale among staff. Critically, communication, commitment, and transparency may enable prison managers to successfully innovate in prisoner management (see Rogers 2003).

Counter to my initial hypothesis, reward power is positively related to institutional commitment (Table 4.2). This finding suggests that the perception of unofficial rewards may improve commitment to the institution. It is plausible that prison workers merely perceive performance to be related to pay—either formally or informally. But the exact implication of a reward power effect is unclear and therefore concerning. Enhanced performance that is not officially recognized as a contributor to promotion is still perceived by prison workers to increase the likelihood of financial gain. This could be interpreted as unofficial and therefore a negative management tool. But it could also be considered as an inevitable result of human-services employment. Intangible qualities—exemplified by strong performance—improve the likelihood of raises. While strictly speaking, informal quid pro quo is not a productive management tool, it may be that workers perceive their own performance on the job to be directly related to improved pay (formally or informally). Under this interpretation, this is not problematic. In addition, it is important to note that reward power is complemented by legitimate, expert, and referent powers (all three of which exhibit a much more robust relationship with institutional commitment). Therefore, the above speculation may not be unlikely. The remaining power, coercive power, as measured through supervision intimidation, is not significantly related to institutional commitment but maintains a negative relationship across all four years. Institutions do not appear to promote intimidation as a suitable power strategy for supervisors. Intimidation does not improve or significantly aggravate the institutional commitment of the prison worker.

Hypothesis 1b: *Well-supervised, treatment-oriented institutions increase commitment levels. Fearful institutions decrease commitment.*

Institutional level contentions do not find as much support. The proposition of this first level-2 hypothesis implies that institutions that have higher supervision marks will result in higher commitment levels among individual workers. Well-supervised, treatment-oriented prisons appear to have no effect on institutional commitment across all four years (not shown). However, fearful institutions, as assessed on the aggregate, are negatively and significantly related to institutional commitment. Institutions that have a higher number of fearful prison workers reduce the institutional commitment of the individual prison worker (Table 4.2). It is not surprising that fearful institutions negatively impact the commitment of the individual worker. Fear is a suitable proxy for perceived safety. Institutions that score higher on aggregate levels of fear presumably are less adequate at protecting prison workers from harm. This inability—or insufficiency—reduces individual commitment levels since the institution is not appearing to provide a base level of care for its employees: freedom from harm.

Given that significance and variation across prisons still exist after the introduction of level-1 variables, it is possible that the selected level-2 variables are insufficient. This analysis suggests that individual level perceptions of the work environment are more salient than institutional level perceptions. Institutions that report higher satisfaction with supervision do not see improved commitment to that institution by the individual worker. Treatment-oriented prisons similarly do not appear to improve the individual's commitment (nor do custody-oriented prisons). The proposition of Hypothesis (1b) argues that treatment-oriented prisons would engender greater meaning in the work and this would increase the individual's commitment to the prison. This does not appear to be the case.

Hypothesis 1c: *Legitimate power has greater influence on commitment in high-security prisons. Reward and referent power have greater influence on commitment in minimum-security prisons.*

In addition, the implication of Hypothesis (1c) is that higher security prisons will rely more on formal (socially approved and officially mandated) types of power while lower security prisons rely on informal and less socially favorable types of power (namely, reward and coercive power). Informal types of power are not found to be related to security level. Hence, Hypothesis (1c) is not supported. However, the impact of legitimate power on institutional commitment is reduced in jails (Table 4.3). This relationship holds across three years. This result indicates that the specific nature of the jail environment is able to buffer the impact of legitimacy on institutional commitment. The jail environment provides much less distraction for prisoners (e.g., less programming). It is possible that institutional commitment is reduced due to the fact that prison workers are less able to control populations through programming, an institutional provision. Notably, analysis from year 2007, finds that the impact of referent power on institutional commitment is increased in jail institutions (Table 4.3). This relationship is not maintained across years of analysis. Nevertheless, due to the unique nature of jails—specifically, limited programming and excessive inactivity—it may be necessary for supervisors to increase their use of referent power strategies to improve employee morale. Analysis from year 2007 also finds that the impact of legitimate power on institutional commitment is decreased in medium-security prisons (Table 4.3). Medium-security prisons may buffer the impact of legitimacy

Table 4.3   Cross-Level Interactions—Power Adoptions and Security Level (*HLM with REML and robust standard errors*)

	Model 3 2007	Model 4 2007	Model 3 2008	Model 3 2009	Model 3 2010
	Coefficient (S. E.)	Coefficient (S. E.)	Coefficient (S. E.)	Coefficient (S. E.)	Coefficient (S. E.)
Cross-Level Interactions					
Referent Power* Jail	0.089** (0.034)	—	—	—	—
Legitimate Power* Medium Security	—	−0.071* (0.033)	—	—	—
Legitimate Power* Jail	—	—	−0.077* (0.040)	−0.136* (0.060)	−0.098* (0.044)
Variance Components	X^2	X^2	X^2	X^2	X^2
U_0	317.827***	318.091***	351.397***	312.169***	531.278***
$U_{Legitimate}$	183.466***	176.305***	144.850*	158.430**	177.261***
U_{Expert}	139.720*	139.711*	—	—	—
$U_{Referent}$	140.121*	146.169*	140.242	157.255**	—

Source: Data from the PSCS, Federal Bureau of Prisons, 2007–2010.
*p<0.05; **p<0.01; ***p<0.001.

due to these institutions' inability to handle populations that are given mid-range sentences. But given the large percentage of drug offenders in federal custody, it is plausible that medium-security prisons see an unusual number of addicts and have an especially difficult time addressing specific population needs. This might reduce their commitment to their overall employer (BOP) and to their specific institution.

It is also important to note that demographics are not consistently significant across years when power adoptions of the institution are considered. Race Black is not significant in 2007 or 2009. Race Black is significant in 2008 and 2010. Gender Female is not significant across all four years. Time at institution and position (line-staff) appear to be relevant across all four years when considering institutional commitment. Organizational factors—including tenure and position—appear to be more salient than demographic factors. I concede that demographics may impact time at institution and position (rank) at institution. Individual level processes predict institutional commitment and largely support the proposition of Hypothesis (1a). Institutional-level processes are less powerful (and less consistently significant across years) and partly support the proposition of Hypothesis (1b). Cross-level interactions are not found to work in the direction or in the institutions promoted by hypothesis (1c). In light of these results, commitment to the institution appears to be largely determined by individual processes. Individual perception (by the prison workers) of the power wielded by supervisors directly impacts institutional commitment in the predicted direction. Institutional-level processes play a much weaker role. Due to the fact that much less of the overall variance is explained at the institutional level, this is not surprising.

POWER AND EFFICACY

I also propose that power adoptions influence the prison worker's ability to effectively manage prisoners. Depending on the type of power strategy, prison workers will perceive more or less ability to handle prisoner populations. This dynamic is perhaps unsurprising but it does suggest that the limited tools available to prison administrators—namely, the restrictions due to finite power strategies—can shape the prison worker's perception of his ability to successfully complete his job. I propose throughout this book that the intelligent employment of power by prison administrators may substantially improve prison management and the prison environment at large. In order to test this proposition that power influences perceived efficacy, I have adopted the following contentions.

Hypothesis 2a: *Legitimate, referent, and expert power improve prison worker ability to manage prisoner populations. Coercive and reward power aggravate perceived effectiveness of prisoner management.*

Hypothesis (2a) predicts that legitimate, referent, and expert power improve prison worker ability to manage prisoner populations. Across all four years of analysis, these three types of power significantly and positively influence prison worker efficacy. These results indicate that skill provision, transparency, and respect empower prison workers and improve their perception of effective prisoner management. Notably, the outcome efficacy is intended to detail successful prisoner management as a complete undertaking—that includes perception of direct inmate management and perception of contribution to the overall environment. It is not possible to disconnect prison workers from prison institutions. The goal of prison work is to manage prisoners, but prison workers also must engage one another (see Table 4.1 for variable composition). As the results indicate, individual prison workers who perceive that they are respected and are given adequate training to handle job responsibilities are more likely to report high levels of efficacy. This suggests that it is possible to empower effective prisoner management. The BOP is able to effectively improve prisoner management through organizational manipulation.

Counter to Hypothesis (2a), coercive power does not aggravate the perception of effectiveness of prisoner management. Perceived intimidation by supervisors improves the perception of efficacy. It is likely that this is less problematic than it appears. Prisons and jails house antisocial populations that are frequently aggressive and impulsive. Effective intimidation by a superior may serve to remind a prison worker of the seriousness of the occupation. Mistakes or oversight may result in serious injury. Intimidation may improve attention to detail and strict oversight—an acceptable version of fear. This strict oversight then improves the ability for the prison worker to effectively manage prisoners. Potentially, intimidation increases the likelihood that strict protocol will be followed, which improves the effect of legitimacy on efficacy. It cannot be assumed, however, that coercive power and intimidation work in such a productive manner. Due to the salience of legitimate, referent, and expert powers it is speculated that coercive power is a complement not an antagonist. Consistent with Hypothesis (2a), reward power is negatively related to efficacy across all four years. But this relationship maintains significance only in year 2009. Reward power implies an informal relationship between the prison worker and his supervisor. This informal perception may aggravate the effectiveness of prisoner management. In terms of inmate management, reward power arguably counters legitimate power. Importantly, however, the effect of reward power fails to consistently reach significance.

Demographics play a much larger role in the outcome efficacy (than in institutional commitment). Race Black is positively and significantly related to efficacy across two years. Black prison workers appear to report an enhanced ability to manage prisoners. Gender Female is negatively and significantly related to efficacy across all four years. Female prison workers appear to report a diminished ability to manage prisoners. Line-staff are negatively related to perception of effective inmate management across all four years of analysis. It is possible that line-staff are somewhat restricted by their ability to shape events and to employ discretion. High school graduates exhibit a negative and significant (across two years) effect on efficacy. Inmate contact increases efficacy across all four years.

Certain populations appear to be better adept at handling inmates. But supervisors also play a substantial role in individual reports of efficacy. Organizational factors are still more powerful and consistent predictors of efficacy than demographics. Manipulating supervision techniques—empowerment through respect and skill acquisition—improves perceived efficacy. Inmate contact also dramatically improves efficacy. Encouragingly, working closely with the prisoner populations increases perception of efficacy.

Hypothesis 2b: *Well-supervised, treatment-oriented institutions improve inmate management. Fearful institutions aggravate inmate management.*

Hypothesis (2b) predicts that aggregate levels of satisfaction with supervision and of treatment orientation will positively impact individual efficacy. As Table 4.4 details, institutional perspectives on supervision and treatment do not appear to have a significant effect on efficacy. Collective opinion of supervision does not appear to impact individual perception of inmate management. Furthermore, treatment orientations (defined as such by the collective) do not appear to significantly improve the prison worker's perception of inmate management. Notably, orientation does have a negative relationship with efficacy across three years (Table 4.4). This suggests, modestly, that custody-oriented prisons exhibit a somewhat aggravating effect on the perception of efficacy. Also counter to Hypothesis (2b), fearful institutions do not appear to contribute to prison worker efficacy. Prisons with increased fear levels do not see efficacy diminish. Hypothesis (2b) proposes that institutional relationships will impact efficacy. Results do not support these claims.

In addition, interpretation of additional model components provides potential insight into security and demographic effects. High security is negatively related to efficacy across all four years (Table 4.4). This relationship is significant in 2010 and significant at a 0.061 level in 2009 (Table 4.4). But it is worth noting that the coefficient for high security in 2008 is very small. High-security prison populations are more dangerous and therefore the ability to manage these populations is likely much more difficult, irrespective of supervision and skill provision. Percent gender female is positively related to efficacy but only significantly (at 0.05 level) in 2009 (Table 4.4). While being female is negatively related to inmate management, prisons with higher percentages of females appear to enhance individual perception of prisoner management. Prison workers report higher levels of effective management with a greater percentage of female coworkers. It is plausible that women workers reduce the aggressive nature of prisoners and of male prison workers and increase the ability to oversee housing units and conduct daily routines.

Hypothesis 2c: *Legitimate and expert powers have greater influence on inmate management in high security. Referent and reward power have greater influence on inmate management in jails and minimum-security institutions.*

Hypothesis (2c) predicts that legitimate power and expert power will have greater influence on efficacy in high-security prisons. Results indicate that this hypothesis is partly supported. The impact of legitimate power on efficacy is increased in high-security institutions across two years (not shown). High security prisons house the most dangerous and aggressive prisoners. In isolation, these prisons diminish the ability for prison workers to effectively

Table 4.4 Efficacy Regressed on Power Adoptions (*HLM with REML and robust standard errors*)

	Model 2 (2007)	Model 2 (2008)	Model 2 (2009)	Model 2 (2010)
	Coefficient (Stand. Error)	Coefficient (Stand. Error)	Coefficient (Stand. Error)	Coefficient (Stand. Error)
Institutional Level				
Intercept	−0.011	−0.018	0.019	0.001
	(0.015)	(0.018)	(0.017)	(0.014)
Supervision	−0.027	−0.013	0.079	0.013
	(0.041)	(0.080)	(0.056)	(0.049)
Orientation	−0.115*	−0.105	−0.108	0.035
	(0.063)	(0.075)	(0.082)	(0.065)
Fear	−0.041	−0.052	0.011	0.004
	(0.246)	(0.051)	(0.045)	(0.032)
Prison Age	0.000	−0.000	−0.000	0.001
	(0.000)	(0.000)	(0.000)	(0.000)
Gender	0.113	0.217	0.507*	0.386
	(0.190)	(0.255)	(0.226)	(0.211)
Race	0.114	0.091	0.253**	−0.118
	(0.106)	(0.146)	(0.092)	(0.100)
High Security	−0.074	−0.000	−0.167	−0.219**
	(0.072)	(0.079)	(0.088)	(0.076)
Individual Level				
Legitimate Power	0.176***	0.243***	0.188***	0.187***
	(0.018)	(0.021)	(0.027)	(0.024)
Coercive Power	0.081***	0.053**	0.085***	0.109***
	(0.015)	(0.019)	(0.021)	(0.015)
Reward Power	−0.024	−0.006	−0.047**	−0.002
	(0.015)	(0.018)	(0.017)	(0.017)
Expert Power	0.160***	0.145***	0.169***	0.206***
	(0.020)	(0.020)	(0.024)	(0.019)
Referent Power	0.237***	0.190***	0.244***	0.180***
	(0.020)	(0.021)	(0.025)	(0.021)
Race Black	0.123***	0.064	0.057	0.165***
	(0.038)	(0.048)	(0.044)	(0.037)
Female	−0.117***	−0.125**	−0.124**	−0.071*
	(0.034)	(0.034)	(0.036)	(0.030)
20+ Years at BOP	0.227***	0.052	0.074	0.071*
	(0.049)	(0.035)	(0.059)	(0.035)
Inmate Contact	0.769***	0.698***	0.783***	0.689***
	(0.066)	(0.068)	(0.077)	(0.070)
High School	−0.110**	0.009	−0.024	−0.120**
	(0.040)	(0.041)	(0.041)	(0.038)
Line Staff	−0.059	−0.048	−0.080*	−0.107**
	(0.034)	(0.039)	(0.038)	(0.032)
Variance Components	X^2	X^2	X^2	X^2
U_0	149.65**	199.478***	118.962	132.149*
$U_{Legitimate}$	—	151.528*	152.306**	183.136***
U_{Expert}	160.491**	—	159.245**	—
$U_{Referent}$	138.690	139.865	—	—
$U_{Coercive}$	—	—	149.185*	—

Source: Data from the PSCS, Federal Bureau of Prisons, 2006–2010.
Note: Models constructed with multiple security level and geographic region controls (not shown but available upon request).
*p<0.05; **p<0.01; ***p<0.001.

manage prisoners. But legitimate power in high-security prisons—presumably, belief in the use of prisons as prescribed by the BOP—appears to counter their natural negative impact. It is beneficial to believe in the role of prison and in the overall goals and purpose of the BOP when working in a high-security prison. Indeed, this belief appears to improve one's perception of prisoner management.

No significant finding for the relationship between expert power and high security is found. Skill provision does not appear to especially improve efficacy in high-security prisons. But the effect of expert power on efficacy is reduced in medium-security prisons for at least one year of analysis (not shown). As suggested earlier, the needs of the medium-security prison population might be insufficiently met by BOP training. Therefore, prison workers feel ill equipped to manage prisoners in these settings. In addition, the effect of referent power is enhanced in minimum security for at least one year of analysis (not shown). Minimum-security prisons are likely to require greater prison worker discretion as perimeter fencing is limited and off-site work may be possible. This framework may increase ambiguity. Referent supervisors may counter this ambiguity by reassuring prison workers of their importance. This result, however, does not reach significance across years.

Individual perception of efficacy appears to be largely reflective of individual processes. Institutional level factors meet directional criteria but fail to reach meaningful significance across years. The propositions of Hypothesis (2b) are rejected. With the exception of coercive power, the propositions of Hypothesis (2a) are confirmed. Rationale for the positive significance of coercive power is stated above and might accurately reflect the nuanced role of supervision in prison environments. In terms of effective management, legitimacy appears to be significantly impacted by high-security prisons. This is directly in line with Hypothesis (2c). Level-2 variance also continues to be significant across prisons. Selected institutional level variables do not entirely explain that variance. Institutional perspectives on peers, charges, and supervisors do not appear to drive individual perceptions of inmate management. Notably, variance due to institutional difference accounts for much smaller proportion of total variance than individual differences.

SUMMARY OF RESULTS: POWER IN PRISON

The results from HLM analysis of survey data from the BOP suggest that legitimate, referent, and expert power positively and significantly impact institutional commitment. (It is important to note that legitimate power is best understood as officially sanctioned BOP policy and generally reflects officially sanctioned treatment of prisoners. Due to issues of collinearity, legitimacy as reflective of perception of fair treatment was not tested in this particular analysis.)

The BOP officially sanctions humane treatment of prisoners and promotes security of staff and prisoners alike. Formal channels, realized through training and alignment with the Bureau of Prisons' philosophy and ideology, appear to affect individual institutional commitment levels. This is not to suggest that informal power strategies are not employed. It is to suggest that formal power strategies appear to be aligned with overall individual institutional management philosophies—and this seems to be reflected by Bureau employees. These results also suggest that the "keeper philosophy"—championed by DiIulio (1987) and reinforced in the BOP manual—applies to the federal prison system (prison workers who subscribe to the belief that loss of liberty is adequate punishment also appear to be more committed to their institution). It should be noted that since the interpretation of power is perceived by prison workers through the actions of supervisors and of the hierarchy in general, these findings indicate that management *can*—through adequate skill provision and attentive supervision—manipulate commitment levels. Moreover, results from four years suggest that organizational factors are more salient in predicting commitment than demographic factors. In the BOP, thereby, management *does* manipulate commitment levels.

From an institutional level, results indicate that prison managers should be concerned about aggregate fear levels of employees. Fearful institutions significantly and negatively impact institutional commitment. It is not surprising that aggregate levels of fear could produce this outcome. Fear of crime generates personal and collective vulnerability partly due to resultant reduced geographical surveillance (Wilson and Kelling 1982). In practice, elevated institutional fear may reduce the likelihood of cell searches, may reduce necessary contact with prisoners, and may reduce rule enforcement. The outcome of these types of negligence ostensibly shift prisoner management to prisoners and cede valuable oversight away from the prison itself. Beyond the reduction in oversight, it is also likely that institutional fear is environmentally and socially addictive. Moderate levels of fear may serve to protect prison workers on the individual level. Elevated levels of institutional fear may serve to undermine adequate management and serve to overestimate risk by prison workers. In the context of this study, fear is considered to be an appropriate proxy for the institutional perspective toward prisoners. Although outside the scope of this inquiry, it is not necessarily the case that high-security prisons are more fearful. Strict protocol and procedures—often witnessed in high-security prisons—may reduce fear levels as workers know how to respond to aggressive and compromising situations and are highly vigilant in maintaining strict oversight (i.e., locking gates).

Results also suggest that significant slope and intercept variation still exist across institutions after the introduction of institutional measures. It is plausible, therefore, that selected level-2 variables are inadequate and unable to capture that variation (but the unexplained variance in these instances is minimal). Institutions may contain a variety of factions that are shielded by institutional averages—especially when assessing general relations within institutions. It is worth mentioning that jail does appear to reduce the positive benefit of legitimate power on institutional commitment (Table 4.3). Minimal programming and increased inmate inactivity may increase the prison workers' perception that jails are improperly run. In addition, the composition of jails is often quite varied and includes high- and low-risk offenders. The combination of this rather diverse offending population could complicate management strategies and create seemingly unnecessary restrictions on low risk offenders in order to maintain uniformity and consistency across management. The confusion on how to appropriately handle a diverse population of offenders may reduce the impact of legitimacy on commitment.

I also propose that power adoptions impact efficacy. My proposal is that formal and constructive forms of power—legitimate, expert, and referent—exhibit positive effects on efficacy. Informal and negative types of power aggravate efficacy. These proposals are largely supported by the analysis. Across four years of analysis, formal and constructive types of power improve prison worker ability to manage prisoner populations. Empowerment through transparency and respect—bestowed after adequate skill provision—improves prison workers' perception of efficacy. It cannot be understated that effective prisoner management includes ability to work within an environment of other prison workers. Therefore the perception that one is a positive influence on that community is wedded to this conceptual arrangement.

Counter to my initial proposal, results indicate that coercive power is not detrimental to efficacy. Perceived intimidation actually improves prison workers' perception of efficacy. This finding reaches significance across all four years. Prisons can be dangerous environments, filled with (potentially) zealously aggressive men and women. Individual fear is not necessarily a liability and intimidation may serve to increase accountability, formality, and rule adherence. It is plausible and not contradictory to suggest that the influence of fear is complex. Fear alerts individuals to danger but also overestimates risk and danger (which ironically may increase likelihood of victimization). In addition, fear of a supervisor is arguably quite different than fear of an inmate. Effective intimidation may merely encourage prison workers to follow protocol and may discourage informal relationship generation. Although ostensibly in opposition to legitimate power, coercive power in this lens may actually permit the unfettered flow of decrees from central command. Coercive power may simply adopt institutional norms to regulate behavior. If those institutional norms are largely antisocial—as may be witnessed within prisoner subcultures—then those antisocial norms will dictate behavior. But if the institutional norms are reflective of legitimacy—which appears to be the case in the federal prison system—then coercive power may simply improve legitimacy. Here, it seems preferable to label coercive as "neutral" rather than "negative."

Institutional level variables appear to complicate the analysis of efficacy. On the individual level, organizational factors (largely relational in nature) predict perception of efficacy. Results suggest that the manipulation of supervision techniques could potentially improve efficacy. But institutional level relational variables—specifically, aggregates of satisfaction with supervision and treatment orientation (also largely relational variables)—do not appear to impact perception of efficacy. It is possible that institutional means are not reflective of within-institutional variation and that aggregations are perhaps not sufficient. Even fearful institutions do not diminish the individual's perception of efficacy. Organizational factors (on the individual level) are powerful predictors of efficacy and relationships improve inmate management. But individual perception of those relationships is far more salient than institutional perception. Moreover, certain populations of prison workers appear to be particularly adept at working with prisoner populations (e.g., Race Black). But inclusion of these control measures does not reduce the effect of power on efficacy. In management settings that appear to encourage individual accountability and minimize collective accountability (e.g., evade blame for unfavorable management outcomes), it is not surprising that individual perceptions are so pertinent.

Cross-level interactions with security suggest that environment may influence the impact of power adoptions on efficacy. The impact of legitimate power on efficacy appears to increase in importance in high-security institutions. Prisoner composition is presumably the most antisocial in these institutions and environmental restrictions are the greatest. Although high-security prisons (at level-2) negatively impact the perception of efficacy, an analysis of cross-level interactions suggests that the effect of legitimacy on efficacy is increased in these same settings. This indicates that prison workers are particularly effective at prisoner management in high-security prisons when they believe in the just authority of the prison institution. The composition of inmates in high-security prisons may aggravate prison workers due to the incessant display of problematic behavior. Taken in isolation, this appears to diminish the worker's perceived ability at managing inmates. But a belief in the prison institution—a belief that prison is the one body that can handle these populations—may actually generate a sense of order and reason in high-security prison work. For example, the worker subscribes to the notion that high-security inmates need to be in prisons with severe restrictions. High-security prisons also have stricter protocols. In order to effectively manage prison populations, the worker simply needs to follow those protocols. Perception of efficacy is thereby increased through subscription to protocol.

EMPOWER, TRAIN, AND LEGITIMIZE

Supervision appears to directly influence prison workers' commitment. Strong supervisors can improve the sense of meaning in prison work (*legitimize*), improve the sense of importance of the prison worker (*empower*), and provide adequate tools to help their employees complete daily tasks (*train*). I have proposed that institutional commitment is an adequate proxy for the prediction of institutional power. Power that has a significant effect on institutional commitment is presumably (and informally) reflective of actual power promoted by the institution. Institutions in the BOP appear to promote legitimate, referent, and expert power strategies. The potential for a changing composition of prisoners makes these fundamental practices essential for safe and effective prison institutions.

Chapter 5

Alienation

Modern prison management arguably desires a degree of alienation from its prison workers. Emotional dissociation may act as a protective factor for correctional officers. Prison work is difficult; prisoner populations are needy, manipulative, and disadvantaged. Indeed, prisons house individuals who have been unable or unwilling to accept membership into collective society. Although widely overused and misused in the past few decades (especially regarding nonviolent drug offenders), forced confinement is ostensibly intended to house populations with irrepressible antisocial tendencies. But this confinement comes with an obligation—morally, on behalf of the imprisoning society—to oversee and care for an "uncontrollable" collection of men and women. It would be unquestionably reckless to openly support further inhumane treatment beyond confinement. More importantly, the *keeper* philosophy strictly endorses the perspective that loss of liberty is adequate punishment. I concede that the widespread adoption of such a position may vary dramatically and may even be somewhat elusive or imaginary. The generation of an entire prison system under a ubiquitous keeper philosophy may be problematic in that an objective and consistent definition for appropriate and fair treatment probably varies. Indeed, what specifically constitutes "loss of liberty"?

But I propose that it is likely that the variation circling this management philosophy is concentrated under less dire practices better understood as benign neglect—or unintended oversight of the nonessential needs of prisoners. This supposition is supported in that no prison facility actively endorses or officially sanctions inhumane treatment of prisoner populations. In essence, officially sanctioned treatment may vary but this variation does not include officially sanctioned mistreatment. In no way do I suggest that mistreatment does not occur. That would be a grand misinterpretation of this supposition. The contention is that mistreatment is neither administratively condoned nor officially recognized as an appropriate prisoner management strategy (and an investigation of prisoner abuse is outside the purview of this book). I find great value in the keeper philosophy not because it presumably ensures fair treatment but because it introduces a nuanced understanding of prison work that reflects prisoner rights *and* prison worker needs. The existence of such an approach implies acute awareness of the potentially intrusive and even overwhelming nature of punitive institutions. Ostensibly, the perspective is a warning to the worker: do not become emotionally involved. The general assumption may be that this serves to ensure fair treatment of prisoners but I reason that it also directly serves to ensure the well-being of the worker.

PRISON: A "PRINCIPLE OF MODERATION"?

Of course, one cannot discount the impact of prisoner composition on the work experience of the correctional officer. Indeed, if prison is used appropriately, prison workers and other members of the state have reason to be offended by prisoner populations. But this same argument ostensibly holds that prison workers are critical to the protection and survival of the state. Individuality and the protection of property and family arguably rely on the mechanisms of social control—a system that, *theoretically*, benefits each member equally and protects each member equally. The nature of such a system allows dutiful members to pursue self-interest within the confines of collective consensus of appropriate behavior. It is, therefore, decidedly in one's best interest as a member of such a state to abide by its general will and to relinquish natural freedom in order that one may join a collective in which all others have also relinquished such freedom (Rousseau 2005 [1762]; Beccaria 1986 [1764]). I may find profound interest in such a compact precisely because it enables me to pursue my individuality *and* it furnishes personal and familial protection. But the benefits of this arrangement are such that one who abides by these conditions may be personally affronted by one who violates them. Indeed, it is logical to presume that the citizens in such a state would harbor great resentment toward such an offender. Thus, their personal anger of the perceived intimate violation could result in horrific punishment. Vengeance becomes disguised as altruism:

> The right to punish has been shifted from vengeance of the sovereign to the defence of society. But it now finds itself recombined with elements so strong that it becomes almost more to be feared. The malefactor has been saved from a threat that is by its very nature excessive, but he is exposed to a penalty that seems to be without bounds. It is a return to a terrible "super-power." It brings with it the need to establish a principle of moderation for the power of punishment. (Foucault 1977, 90)

Clearly, the state would not survive such brutal public punishment even in defense of such a cherished reality. Brutality would engender fear as opposed to satisfaction, and the state itself—far from positioning itself as protector of the individual—would appear vulgar, tyrannical, and vicious. Perhaps by fortune, the prison institution arguably solves this dilemma. Prison provides this "principle of moderation." Imprisonment can exist outside the public eye but not beyond the public imagination. Prison serves adequately to deter both by perception and (presumably) by reality.

I engage in this discussion because it advocates for our sincere desire for the prison institution as our place of punishment and also illustrates the complex, necessary, and laudatory role of prison work. Prison workers must confront this reality with compassion and without judgment. This argument does not suggest that prison is applied fairly or adequately; nor does it suggest that progression and reformation of current incarceration practices are not necessary. Rather, this proposition merely illustrates a social desire for a principle of moderation. Of course, and this is an important distinction, it is far easier to make an argument for prisons *in general* than it is to make an argument for the current *practice* of imprisonment and the current size of the prison population. Yet, I believe that it is misguided to assume that the current practice of imprisonment is a result of the inevitable nature of prison itself. Arguably, the dramatic rise in imprisonment over the past three decades may be explained by a general shift in criminal justice policy rather than any substantial increase in crime (Blumstein and Beck 1999; National Research Council 2014). The resultant implication is not that prisons fail but that our reliance on prison to solve considerable social ills is foolhardy. I view abolitionists (e.g., Davis 2003) as champions of a much-needed reform of current imprisonment practices and policies rather than rigidly attached to a particular extreme ideology. If it is an ideological stance then I fear that abolitionists minimize one central, and perhaps uncomfortable, reality: actors do exist who frighten the general public and who are ill fit for general society.

Since there are those whom we fear, I see it as logical that prison exist for at least a subset of offenders. But this theoretical argument for prison cannot be made without Freudian justice: "a law once made will not be broken in favour of an individual" (Freud 1961 [1930], 49). No citizen can be above the law. Otherwise the collective does not consistently and objectively remove citizens from the state.

REASONABLE AND UNREASONABLE ALIENATION?

Due to the composition of prisoners and the general practice of placing the most dangerous and the most antisocial in detention centers (admittedly, among those who are far from dangerous), prison workers face a difficult balancing act. The actions of select prisoners could deeply offend the workers who have willfully decided to abide by the mutually beneficial social compact. But as DiIulio (1987, 170) observes: "if prison workers were upset or became angry every time they passed by a convicted murderer or rapist they would be unable to perform their duties properly." Their role, indeed their duty, is not to stand in judgment of their charges. Instead, entrance into prison becomes time zero: "a prisoner should be treated humanely and in accordance with how he behaves inside the institution. Even the most heinous offender is to be treated with respect and given privileges if he behaves well once behind the walls" (DiIulio 1987, 167). Irrespective of guilt or prior behaviors, the correctional officer is expected to suspend emotional connection, in effect suspend judgment, in order to create a safe and humane prison environment.

In theory, thereby, increased professionalism increases the effectiveness of prison management and may increase the *legitimate* authority of the correctional officer. But it also arguably distances the correctional officer from his charges, perhaps even from his immediate environment. Seasoned professionalism may appear to be "callous" or "unfeeling" behavior (DiIulio 1987, 170) because this variety of professionalism is intended to be unfeeling and, in essence, survives and effectively manages because it is dissociated. Consequently, the presented social self—the self witnessed by the prison population—is encouraged to be static, unemotional, objectively fair, and consistent. This custom, while potentially harboring great utility, may have a variety of consequences. But this was not always the demeanor of prison workers. Lombardo (1989) adeptly describes the change in correctional officer role perception as directives and rule adherence became much more critical in order maintenance as the 1970s moved into the 1980s.

Prison environments, nudged by management philosophy, do appear suitable for employee alienation. Indeed, prison administrators arguably endorse dissociation from prisoners. But the focus of this discussion has largely diagrammed the relationship between the prison worker and the prisoner and has neglected to illustrate the nuanced bond the prison worker may have with the prison institution itself. I propose that the nature of prison management itself alienates the prison worker from the prison institution. In this regard, the prison worker perceives to be alienated from supervisors and administrators—perceives to be dissociated from actively shaping the work environment. Of course, alienation between worker and employer is an ambiguous idea often derived from factory analogy—suggesting the reclassification and transformation of abstract human worth into mechanical means reflective of burgeoning industrialization. But prison workers do not make products, and transferring their labor into an analogy of production ostensibly perpetuates disadvantage and illustrates social inadequacy and vulgarity in

understanding prisoners and in understanding prison work. Although complicated in these origins and in connotation, several notable clarifications have
been able to transfer these early abstractions into clear academic categories
that are advantageous here and do not bleed across dissimilar processes
(Seeman 1959; Aiken and Hage 1966; Dean 1961). Specifically, Seeman
(1959) defines alienation through five general areas: powerlessness, meaninglessness, normlessness, isolation, and self-estrangement. This favorable
arrangement—favorable due to its precision and sophistication—is adopted
here. Notably, Poole and Regoli (1981) adopted Seeman's (1959) approach
in the assessment of alienation among correctional officers in a maximum-
security prison in the Midwest. Their findings indicated a strong sense of
alienation within correctional officer ranks but the impact of that alienation
was not directly addressed.

POWERLESSNESS

The central goal of prison management arguably promotes powerlessness of
employees. Security is the central goal: "Security-conscious prison management will yield more in the way of prison order, amenity, and service than
less dedicated, more lax prison management; in short, prison management
matters" (DiIulio 1987, 256). A strict security focus endorses central command, strict rule adherence, and environmental control. Independent actions
dilute the efficiency of the chain of command and provide for unpredictable
outcomes. The likelihood of independent decision-making in prisons is perhaps unlikely (or at least minimized). As Poole and Regoli (1981) contend:
"the work behavior of the guard is, to a great extent, a function of the decisions and actions of others occupying subordinate, as well as superordinate
positions in the correctional institution. For these reasons powerlessness
would appear to be a fundamental feature of the guard's work experience"
(256). Lombardo (1989, 145) illustrates a form of powerlessness that revolves
around minimal institutional support. Not only do guards often feel unsupported by the hierarchy, but this lack of support translates into lack of trust or
effectiveness at role fulfillment: "officers are also concerned that they lack the
responsibility and decision-making power necessary to contribute effectively
to their work environment" (Lombardo 1989, 145). Although on the front
lines of prison management, line-staff at Auburn Prison in the 1970s voiced
an inability to shape, modify, and adjust standard practices even though possessing requisite and uniquely germane experiences (Lombardo 1989).

It is not clear that autonomy is without merits in the detention center.
Barring emergencies, discretion and autonomy may play a critical role in
efficient and productive prison management. Discretion does not require

mayhem. Strong centralized authority may still provide adequate leadership and input from subordinate officers and create an environment that embraces autonomy—while also enforcing uniformity. In their discussion of alienation, Aiken and Hage (1966, 498) illustrate two varieties of centralization: "First, organizations vary in the extent to which members are assigned tasks and then provided with the freedom to implement them without interruption from superiors. . . . A second, and equally important, aspect of the distribution of power is the degree to which staff members participate in setting the goals and policies of the entire organization." Indeed, there is sufficient room for correctional agencies to maintain security-focused order and allow for officer autonomy (which may improve morale). It is not necessary for officers to make decisions that depart from the mission of the prison, nor act outside the prescriptions of central command. The reduction of alienation requires communication and acknowledgement of communication between management and line-staff. Relative to the alienation spectrum, powerlessness stands in opposition to empowerment. This use of powerlessness reflects Seeman's (1959, 784, italics in original) definition: "*the expectancy or probability held by the individual that his own behavior cannot determine the occurrence of the outcomes, or reinforcements, he seeks.*" The ability to structure the environment and the mission of the correctional facility may empower the correctional officer and reduce the sense of powerlessness. Superior training may increase the effectiveness of correctional line-staff; thereby, improving the trust by management in their efficacy of order maintenance and rule enforcement.

Measuring Powerlessness

The powerlessness measure reflects the individual prison worker's perception that she is able to shape outcomes within the institutional setting and that change is indeed possible. Implicitly, therefore, power indicates discretion. But the environment itself has to permit the individual actor to shape it—indeed, the environment itself must welcome some form of change or adaptation in order that power can be exhibited. Thereby, power is not only a reflection of the individual's perception that she may shape her role within the larger institution and conduct her daily operational duties with a moderate degree of flexibility but that the system itself welcomes such individuality and is conducive to changing procedures at the bequest of individual workers. This does not imply that the individuals who express a great deal of power are subversive or somehow able to dictate outcomes, outside of the Bureau of Prisons doctrine. As should be clear by the operationalization of powerlessness (Table 5.1), this measure largely demonstrates the degree to which the prison worker perceives discretion within the confines of the job and whether

Table 5.1 Specified Construction of Dependent Variables and Alienation Measures
(Alpha scores for 2007, 2008, 2009, 2010; Factor loading for correlation with latent variable, 2007)

	Alpha Scores (2007, 2008, 2009, 2010)	Factor Loading (Year 2007)
Efficacy***		
Hardening*	0.6927, 0.6918, 0.6969, 0.6855	
A feeling that you have become harsh toward people since you took this job		0.8437
A feeling of being emotionally drained at the end of the workday.		0.7466
A feeling that you treat some inmates as if they were impersonal objects.		0.7702
Normlessness*	0.6119, 0.6360, 0.6476, 0.6200	
Formal authority is not clear		0.6093
I get information that helps me do my job better**		0.7706
I communicate effectively with coworkers (never/all the time)**		0.6028
I know what supervisor expects of me**		0.7551
Powerlessness*	0.6538, 0.6423, 0.6770, 0.6819	
I have lots of say so over my job**		0.6534
Change is not possible here		0.8235
No influence on what goes on in BOP		0.8271
Meaninglessness*	0.6411, 0.6422, 0.6538, 0.6701	
Promotions and performance are unrelated		0.6908
Authority is clearly delegated**		0.6239
My job is interesting to me**		0.6650
My hard work will be recognized**		0.7892
Isolation*	0.7541, 0.7631, 0.7891, 0.7997	
My ideas and opinions are valued**		0.7304
I feel that I work well with others**		0.8782
I communicate effectively with coworkers**		0.8751
Self-Estrangement*	0.8715, 0.8696, 0.8794, 0.8785	
My BOP jobs is usually worthwhile**		0.9416
My BOP job suits me very well**		0.9416

Source: Data from the PSCS, Federal Bureau of Prisons, 2007–2010.
*Each response scaled seven points from "strongly disagree" to "strongly agree".
**Reverse Coded.
***See Table 4.1 for alpha scores and factor loading.
All constructed measures load sufficiently onto a single factor for every year (2007 shown).

or not this same prison worker perceives that the institution can change and that BOP responds to individual concerns or suggestions.

MEANINGLESSNESS

Security is critical to prisoner management. But it is unclear if security-focused prisons automatically generate a sense of meaning for prison workers. DiIulio (1987, 256) insists: "Prison workers can simultaneously share a sense of mission, identify with each other, care about the inmates, and perform well a vital service to the people of the law-abiding and tax-paying community." But practice may trump optimism in this model. In practice, this "paramilitary prison bureaucracy" may not resemble the efficiency and the intimacy of the strict military model. This prison model may effectively combat violent and aggressive charges but prisons are not military bases. A fair comparison of workforces would require equal work: the day-to-day supervision of prisoners would need to reflect the altruistic sense of importance and duty that the military provides. In addition, cultural perceptions of military personnel would also need to mirror cultural perceptions of correctional officers. It is admitted that security concerns are vital to successful prison management—as they are to successful military operations. But, unlike military personnel, it is less clear that conflict events such as prison riots would automatically increase sympathies for correctional officers. The public is likely to first consider prisoners when considering prisons and only abstractly consider prison workers within the confines of the institution of the prison.

However, by the mere fact of its continued existence and frequent employment in the administering of punishment, forced confinement is a reasonable and rational management solution for antisocial populations. It is reasonable since it suggests that the larger community and the citizenry at large willfully accept the use of prison. Indeed, the removal of the incorrigibles is publicly approved—and warrants public approval. But adequate concern for those who oversee those incorrigibles is less sympathetic. It appears to be possible to favor the use of prison and simultaneously hijack meaning from those who supervise prisoners: "[f]eeling that they are abused by inmates, unappreciated by superiors, unsupported by colleagues, guards tend to think they are fighting a lost cause" (Poole and Regoli 1981, 258). Practice may actually contradict DiIulio's optimistic assertion regarding meaning. Prison management may work at ensuring safe prisons, but it does not necessarily follow that these same prisons engender meaning.

Meaninglessness is greater than simply the belief that automatons could perform the tasks of line-staff. Seeman (1959, 786, italics in original) insists: "one might operationalize [meaninglessness] by focusing upon the fact that it is characterized by *low expectancy that satisfactory predictions about future outcomes of behavior can be made.*" This definition illustrates meaninglessness in an absolute sense—in which the actor becomes removed from the fundamental shaping of events. Acute appreciation and comprehension of the world may actually detail helplessness. This sensitive actor understands the futility in preventing and igniting specific courses of action. I contend that the troubling conflict between the necessary role of prison, the apparent failure of prison, and the underappreciated role of the prison worker fosters meaninglessness. Remarkably, the individual is not socially or publicly valued for his contribution but the work that is his contribution is of acute value and is deemed unequivocally necessary. Sadly, greater knowledge and work experience may only aggravate this sense of meaninglessness or lack of control for the prison worker (e.g., "fighting a lost cause"). Prisoners leave and return to prison at an astonishingly high rate (Pew Center on the States 2011); prisoners resemble one another and little appears to be affecting change on the outside or on the inside. This helplessness is arguably central to the experience of prison work.

Lack of sympathetic supervision may only further the meaninglessness in the oversight of inmates. A strict hierarchical order will not automatically inject meaning into prison work—meaning of purpose, and of importance. The removal of antisocial actors is critical to social order (and in this way meaningful), but the care of those who have failed to care for others, as well as the cultural perspectives of and requirements for that care, are more nuanced. Regardless of effort, little may be done to affect change. The perception of prison work from the public, from prison administrators, and from charges may work in tandem to create a grand sense of meaninglessness in the profession of prisoner watching.

Measuring Meaninglessness

The meaninglessness measure indicates that the prison worker perceives the work as possessing very little intrinsic value with a low expectation that on-the-job performance will result in promotion (Table 5.1). The latent construct of meaninglessness is nuanced, layered. The central component to this constructed measure recognizes that investment in the work will be perceived favorably by supervisors and by the prison administration in general. Meaningful work consists of attentive supervision that recognizes sacrifice and hard work. But this measure also suggests that the job itself offers daily nourishment and sates a more abstract need for suitable and challenging employment. Presumably, if the job is perceived to be interesting, then the worker is invested and finds value in daily interactions and tasks.

NORMLESSNESS

Durkheim (1951 [1897]) champions the notion that only human society may restrain, or limit, human appetite. Animal appetites are naturally limited and restrained by sustenance. A tired and full animal is without desire. Natural limits cannot restrain the reflective power of the human animal. Unrestrained wants imagined through reflection breed unhappiness. Accordingly, since the individual would never accept an unjust rule over her—rule that could be manipulated to individual wills—she will only accept society to regulate her wants. This acceptance allows the individual to know where she fits, what is appropriate for her to want, and what should be considered unreasonable. This acceptance also permits society's morality to gain hold of the individual. As Durkheim insists, society makes the individual moral. Breaks in the hold of society lead to deviance as the individual no longer understands where she fits and may no longer be able to satisfy her customary needs. The realized comfort and happiness in the individual—according to the normlessness, or anomic, argument—rests in the individual knowing where she fits and what is reasonable to desire. This is her acquired normative behavior. According to the individual, violation of this behavior should result in punishment, and breaks in her bonds to society will confuse what this normative behavior actually is.

Relevant to the correctional facility, understanding institutional norms allows correctional officers to appreciate their role and to administer punishment reflective of the management. In practice, this may erode as the role of prison becomes more varied. Although DiIulio (1987) insists that only prison can simultaneously fulfill all four goals of punishment, the result of the implementation of ostensibly conflicting goals may confuse appropriate responses to inmate behaviors (Poole and Regoli 1981). It may be reasonable to presume that correctional officers perceive security as the chief concern while differing in their beliefs on what types of behavior threaten the secure fabric of the correctional setting. The administering of oversight may require a balancing act—but may also involve a devaluation in normative rules:

> [i]f guards were to enforce the rules by formally reporting all inmate infractions, the relatively high frequency of disciplinary response would likely be viewed by superiors as evidence of poor work performance or an inability to handle inmates. Conversely, if they were discovered exercising undue discretion or overlooking infractions, guards would be subject themselves to disciplinary sanctions. (Poole and Regoli 1981, 257)

Even though the balancing act may be achieved through experience, there may not exist normative responses to specific incidents. It may then be perceived by the actor that the outcome, irrespective of the process, will result in favorable or unfavorable management review. Merton (1938) defined innovation as the rejection of appropriate means to pursue cultural goals. The actor pursues the cultural goal of the American Dream, but rejects the socially appropriate, or legal, means to achieve that goal. Seeman (1959) assumes a similar position. Normlessness, or anomie, occurs when "there is a high expectancy that socially unapproved behaviors are required to achieve given goals" (Seeman 1959, 788). But this definition will not suffice. It is possible that this limitation precludes the possibility that normlessness merely frees the actor to engage in *any* behavior that will result in a favorable outcome. The behavior need not be actively unapproved. The behavior only needs to be unregulated. This allows the possibility that the officer, irrespective of management, may pursue acceptable or unacceptable rule enforcement—whichever is more readily available in any given situation.

This variety of normlessness devalues process—a process potentially invested in the *keeper* model—in favor of the outcome (thus eliminating the communal sense of societal purpose of forced confinement). This type of alienation will distance the correctional officer from the governing body and loosen his grasp of appropriate care for prisoners. Tragically, it is not possible to disregard the management of prisoners and fully embrace the purpose of prison (according to the social contract and justice). Hence, alienation of this sort may have a dramatic impact on the life and work ethic of the correctional officer. The officer no longer knows where he fits, what behavior is appropriate, and the alienation allows for deviation from socially appropriate behaviors.

Measuring Normlessness

Normlessness indicates that the prison worker is unclear of protocol and does not readily understand supervisory expectations (see Table 5.1). Central to this concept is failed communication. This could be perceived as the inability for the institution itself to relay its message to its workers. Due to the complexity of managing prisoners, administrators and direct supervisors may appear to contradict one another in perceived expectations. An inability to access the institution's normative code increases the likelihood that the individual generates his own code that does not limit, restrict, or outlaw any particular type of behavior or any particular course of action. Extreme normlessness merely favors outcomes—it is not restricted to professional or ethical conduct. Concern over job security trumps ethical or professional demeanor. Indeed, in this regard, the administration has failed to communicate expectations *and* has failed to ensure that those expectations are not contradicted through practice (e.g., inconsistent infraction enforcement).

ISOLATION

Durkheim (1951 [1897]) argued that reduced social integration increased individual self-interest, weakened communal restraint, and allowed for deviance. The detachment from society created an inability to regulate oneself. Similar to the above discussion of anomie, the isolated individual is an unhappy and deviant individual for society is unable to limit her wants. Employing similar arguments, Faris and Dunham (1939) argued that weak social integration increased social isolation by reducing effective communal interaction. Shaw and McKay (1942) claimed a similar phenomenon: neighborhood structural factors, such as low income, population heterogeneity, and residential turnover, could weaken informal social controls and subsequently increase health epidemics and crime rates. The failure of the community to integrate the individual frees her from its moral grasp and permits deviance. Isolation from the community—physically or emotionally—will increase individual purpose and decrease the collective, or altruistic, drive. In one sense, normlessness leads to isolation: "In attempting to minimize their own personal risk and trouble, guards come to define their roles in a highly individualized manner, essentially detached from the overall institutional concerns" (Poole and Regoli 1981, 258). And this isolation results in a breakdown in communal control:

> the individualization of the guard's role serves to isolate the guards from one another so they cannot depend on the help or cooperation of colleagues. Unable to rely on fellow officers, guards make their own accommodations on the tiers to ensure their own safety and security. In short, guards maintain a defensive posture in the social organization of the prison, working neither for the administrators nor for the inmates but for themselves. (Poole and Regoli 1981, 258–259)

Social isolation permits the correctional officer to deviate from culturally appropriate norms—norms that the prison administrators promote. This isolation further alienates the officer from communal connection, from responsibility outside her own immediate tasks, and renders the fabric of the correctional employee community fractured.

Measuring Isolation

Isolation indicates that the prison worker is socially removed from his peers and does not feel as though he is an active and important part of the environment (see Table 5.1). He is unable to effectively communicate with his coworkers and he perceives that his environment—his supervisors, his peers—does not respect his ideas or his perspectives. In essence, he is socially outcast from the embrace of the community of which he is an integral part. Due to management practices that often target individual blame rather than collective accountability, this perspective contends that it is likely that individual workers do not perceive that the prison administration or their direct supervisors value their contributions.

SELF-ESTRANGEMENT

The reduction of the value of labor in and of itself—that the work completed provides little satisfaction beyond its completion—increases the possibility of self-estrangement (Seeman 1959). This variety of alienation, the removal of "intrinsically rewarding experiences" (Poole and Regoli 1981, 259), breeds actors that are largely uninterested in the overall function of the host, endeavor little to produce a more effective workplace, and desire little but uneventful tours. As Poole and Regoli (1981, 259) contend:

> [The correctional officer] feels little pride in his work since the public imbues the job with such negative attributes. He feels his work is underappreciated by his superiors since they seem to show greater concern for the interests of the inmates. And since his immediate associates cannot be counted on, he enjoys no spirit of teamwork. These conditions create few incentives for the infusion of the worker's self in his work and consequently results in self-estrangement.

This self-estranged correctional officer is arguably a liability for the facility. His disinterest in the well-being of his host potentially dismantles, or at least disrupts, the cohesion of proper management. The isolation from the community combines with little sense of value of the labor and dissolves investment in what is essentially team-oriented labor. It is conceded that the factory laborer who is easily replaced and finds minimal merit in the factory employ costs factory owners only the rate of his productivity—his true self-estrangement burdens only himself and his pursuit of happiness. To avoid being fired, however, he arguably works reasonably efficiently without garnering any sense of value from the process. But human services— especially those charged with the management of unruly and unpredictable populations—require an injection of trust in the atmosphere in order to temper aggressive emergencies. The question is whether self-estrangement is an inevitable outcome of prison management—and if so, what impact would this self-estrangement have on effective inmate oversight. Seeman (1959, 790) defines self-estrangement as: "the degree of dependence of the given behavior upon anticipated future rewards." It is not clear that a strict focus on anticipated future rewards reduces productivity or security in prison environments. If the salary is valued adequately then even the most estranged will strive for safe tours—no matter their emotional connection to the prison environment. This variety of alienation assumes negative impacts on the perception of inmates and fellow officers—begging the inquiry not only into the validity of this claim but also into the potential population variation in susceptibility to this phenomena.

Measuring Self-Estrangement

Given the restrictions due to the prison environment and perhaps necessary management perspectives, the likelihood that prison workers perceive their jobs as intrinsically rewarding and deeply reflective as who they are as individuals and who they are as humans is perhaps rather low. This could be an indication that the public does not grant prison workers due respect and fails to honor their sacrifice. This measure is captured as a combination of job suitability and job satisfaction (see Table 5.1).

OVERALL INFERENCES

The above discussion of alienation suggests not only that the prison environment will be shaped by alienation but also that this alienation may have diverse impacts on the effectiveness of prisoner management. Although necessary for safe prisons, current management strategies may have unhelpful effects on prison work and this will be most pronounced in high-security prisons where discretion is limited and formal rule adherence is maximized. To be direct, I largely infer that alienation reduces prison worker ability to manage prisoners and that this impact will be greatest in high security prisons. I also infer that alienation hardens prison workers and that high-security prisons will increase this hardening and low-security prisons will decrease this hardening.

A COMMENT ON BURNOUT

Population-specific human-service environments arguably expose workers to moderate or even severe levels of uniformity in the presentation of client needs. Due to this potential consistency, perspectives toward objectively extreme conditions may be subjectively mollified by excessive exposure. Human-service environments, especially those that serve at-risk men and women, increase the risk of deleterious effects on tenured staff, perhaps even without worker acknowledgement (see Maslach 1978; Maslach and Jackson

1981). Often labeled "burnout," this impact may increase substance use, depression, or even simple emotional dissonance (Maslach, Schaufeli, and Leiter 2001). Burnout may play a direct role in correctional officer perception of his work environment and his charges. Specifically, the Maslach and Jackson (1981) perspective illustrates the value of exhaustion, depersonalization, and inefficacy. But I propose that even though the latent construct "burnout" may be a worthwhile pursuit as an *outcome* (due to the identifiable restrictions of certain types of environments), its operationalization is often misleading and problematic. Importantly, I do believe that the proper characterization of environments conducive to ill emotional health is necessary. And I believe that the intention of the burnout construct is well placed. But, with regard to the specifics of prison environments, I doubt its effective relevance as currently conceived.

Of course, this discussion is incomplete without a least a cursory detail of the burnout construct. Burnout is particularly relevant to professional occupations that supply direct emotional support to at-risk populations. Ostensibly, thereby, the inclusion of burnout into this theoretical discussion is generally considered merited as correctional officers are unable to evade continual contact with a potentially manipulative and certainly needy population of men and women and these same officers often are required to provide, at the minimum, some level of personal care (see Lombardo 1989). Admittedly, burnout specifically illustrates the personal suffering of human-service workers and their respective responses to stress and adversity. But it does not adequately grant insight into critical and specific processes—beyond the speculation of heightened emotion—that lend themselves toward such an outcome. In response, I contend that alienation is preferable in that it (1) defines a theoretical argument that reflects the necessary (and potentially harmful) components of prison management and (2) it does not combine potentially dissimilar elements into a single measure. This is not to suggest that the latent concept of burnout is not advantageous or valuable. But burnout is largely considered through Maslach and Jackson's (1981) burnout inventory. This inventory is the most widely used measure and it is the only measure that is continually tested to measure burnout among correctional officers. But as conceived by Maslach and Jackson (1981), I propose that burnout is inadequate as a predictor and it is insufficient as an outcome.

The Maslach and Jackson (1981) construction does not further our inquiry into the arguably essential nature of prison environments. I admit that the conceptualization is not without intrigue—"depersonalization" is directly related to alienation from work. But I have proposed that dissociation from prisoners is not necessarily a negative outcome of prison work. Since Maslach et al. (2001, 403) define depersonalization as: "An attempt to put distance between oneself and service recipients by actively ignoring the qualities that make them unique and engaging people," I admit that this outcome is decidedly undesirable. In fact, I find no evidence that burnout is a desirable outcome. But I cannot discount the fact that dissociation (specifically from prisoners) may be beneficial to prison work. A degree of depersonalization—as defined by Maslach and Jackson (1981)—might actually increase the effectiveness of the correctional officer, specifically in the employment of legitimate power and perceived objective fairness. Taken to its extreme, dissociation as objectification is an undesirable outcome. But dissociation is not necessarily extreme and is therefore not necessarily undesirable. The cornerstone of their burnout measure appears to be unequivocally negative to Maslach and Jackson (1981). But there is a reality of prison work that may require a degree of dissociation. Prisons forcibly detain men and women that society ostensibly fears. First contact, and even continual contact, with inmates might be unsettling:

> when correctional workers begin taking responsibility for their actions, they usually become emotionally involved in maintaining respect for their position. But inmates provide a direct challenge to their authority and because of the official rules and regulations governing correctional workers' conduct toward inmates, the workers find themselves in a position where they must become psychologically immune from the batter of verbal assaults they receive . . . new correctional officers soon come to see that their lot is with fellow workers, and they define others as enemies. (Regoli, Poole, and Schrink 1979, 185)

No set of standards will reduce unfavorable verbal assaults. But persistent mockery can affect attitude. In order to successfully navigate such a system, a certain level of "thick skin" may be necessary. I do not propose that objectification is therefore advantageous or preferable in prison environments. I do propose, however, that theoretical arguments should clearly dictate analysis and leave room for a potentially complex and nuanced reality. This is an attempt to logically assess genuine environmental factors that could shape the experience for correctional officers. Regardless of connotation, mild depersonalization may be essential to prison operations and effective population management. Of course, overlooking conditions that could inflict painful outcomes would undermine the keeper philosophy (therefore, objectification as an example of extreme dissociation must be theoretically unfavorable). Prison itself is punishment and perhaps it does not need to provide a greater, and unjustified, source of anguish. But what measureable quality is counter to "depersonalization" and appropriate for prison officers' conduct?

Of course, the concern is not limited to this one component. Maslach and Jackson (1981) combine depersonalization with exhaustion and inefficacy to construct their completed burnout measure. But these are potentially distinct processes that are better considered in their parts. It is plausible that the prison worker may be less exhausted *and* more impersonal *and* perceive that he is more effective at prisoner management. The potential for the components to diverge in value is substantial. Indeed, the measure itself does not seem reasonable as a single measure. It may be better to analyze what type of officer prisons make rather than assuming that prisons should make certain types of officers. The dangerous conclusion of the burnout literature is that institutions generate horrific outcomes because of their *nature* yet that very nature is ill-defined or overlooked completely.

There is arguably no environment like the prison. It is likely that prisoners neither appreciate correctional officers nor appreciate prison, and it is not productive nor is it possible to sanction "verbal assaults" or other harmless yet unsettling and frequent behaviors. Research, notably, has evaluated the effect of aggressive behavior within other professional occupations and the supposition generally seems to surface that prison work must be comparable to other types of work since, presumably, other types of work also serve needy, disadvantaged, and volatile populations. Perhaps the most promising comparison with the present work assesses violence against nurses in hospitals (e.g., Jackson, Clare, and Mannix 2002; Camerino et al. 2007). I willingly concede that workplace violence may impact "recruitment and retention" (Jackson, Clare, and Mannix 2002). But this research does not address alienation and power adoptions of nurses and the subsequent impact on efficacy or on commitment. In addition, it is unclear that nurses select into their field with the knowledge that their employment deals with violent populations. Admission to hospitals may require injury or illness but it does not require a social consensus that (behaviorally) one is insufficiently equipped to safely operate unsupervised. The same case cannot be made for prison workers. The work itself and selection into the field implicitly accept this unique level of oversight. In this regard, comparisons across security level may be more valuable than comparisons to nonequivalent work environments. Minimum-security prisons often do not even have fences (USDOJ 2011) and inmates are often permitted work release. High-security prisons control movement and have towers and steep perimeter fences. Rather than attempting to force two populations together that are unalike (for selection *and* environmental reasons), it may be preferable to assess differences within and across institutions that share the same "label" but might operate very differently internally.

The theoretical construct "burnout" is an insufficient measure for the prison environment. Burnout does not adequately address the complexity in effective prison management. I have argued that it inappropriately assigns negative value to potential protective factors and would undermine the nuance of prison management. Alienation reasonably subsumes—where appropriate—and far exceeds the main tenets of burnout by illustrating and diagramming a theoretical perspective of prison management. In addition, recent ethnographic work strongly endorses the central themes of alienation (Tracy 2004, 2008; Tracy and Scott 2006). The research indicates the importance of "powerlessness," lack of appreciation by the general public (within law enforcement), and emotional exhaustion. But research to date is missing a strong organizing principle that reflects the theoretical implications of prison management and synthesizes processes into an impactful and meaningful measure. I propose that the selected measures of alienation in this study provide a more complete, and theoretically justifiable, assessment of the complicated and oft underappreciated role of the correctional officer.

EFFICACY IN PRISONER MANAGEMENT
AND EMOTIONAL HARDENING

In testing the effects of alienation, I apply the same outcome measure of efficacy as illustrated in Chapter 4 (see Table 4.1). This outcome is critical in order to illustrate the negative impact that alienation measures have on the perception of effective prisoner management. I also generate a measure ("hardening") to capture early signs of "dehumanizing" factors potentially present in prison workers. Due to the complexity of prison work, it is important to note that these two outcomes are not combined as suggested in the burnout literature. Indeed, these are unique outcomes that capture and measure latent phenomenon. Since the Prison Climate Social Survey is self-reported, these measures implicitly suggest that the prison worker is somewhat aware of his emotional hardening. By responding favorably to "hardening" components, prison workers admit that: "they have become harsh"; they "[feel] emotionally drained"; and they "[feel] as though they treat some inmates as if they were impersonal objects" (see Table 5.1).

But dissociation does not necessarily require objectification. These processes are potentially distinct—much as a therapist views her patient from a removed location but does not perceive the patient as an impersonal object. Similarly, the emotional distance of the prison worker may be necessary and even desirable but this does not necessarily result in impersonal objectification. I propose that impersonal objectification removes—or at least skews— the clear vision of the prison worker. In this lens, it is likely that essential needs become nonessential needs and the keeper philosophy is challenged or undermined. I do not propose that extreme dissociation is beneficial. In fact, I find heightened dissociation to be detrimental. The proposed contention is that mild dissociation from potentially antisocial populations is beneficial since it does not desensitize the prison worker to the needs of the prison population and does not emotionally compromise his oversight. More importantly, however, I generated a hardening variable that captures three highly related phenomenon (and addresses the concerns listed in earlier sections): emotional exhaustion of the self, hardening toward the world in general, and perceived hardening toward his immediate environment. These three processes work in tandem and are theoretically viable as components of one measure. The worker perceives growing exhaustion, global callousness, and objectification. As designed and presented here, "hardening" is a decidedly negative outcome that clearly indicates dissociation as problematic to the prisoner in terms of his objectification *and* to the prison worker in terms of his perception toward his self and his primary and secondary environments. Lastly, it cannot be overstated that the prison worker perceives his alienation (the key predictor of hardening) by way of the prison administration—through his perception of his direct and indirect supervision. Therefore, in this regard, he is largely a product of a potentially malleable environment.

In the following two sections, I provide a technical account of the analytical results regarding alienation measures. These sections allow the reader direct insight into specific findings of this study and conclusions thereby later drawn.

RESULTS: ALIENATION AND EFFICACY

I generated six alienation measures (Table 5.1). Prior to analysis, however, a few issues of correlation needed to be addressed. Alienation measures are highly correlated. Given the theoretical overlap, this is not terribly surprising. Alienation constructions are critical to a latent quality of prisons. But it is not overly concerning that its individual parts are highly related. Indeed, they depict highly similar processes. But it is necessary to run separate analyses for each measure (see Chapter 3 for specifics of the analytical approach).

Hypothesis 3a: *Alienation reduces prison worker ability to manage prisoners.*

I first propose that alienation reduces the prison worker's ability to manage prisoners. Across all four years of analysis, alienation significantly and negatively relates to efficacy. The strength of the effect of alienation on efficacy, evidenced by significant variation in its slope across institutions and across four years, also varies by institution. Likewise, powerlessness, meaninglessness, normlessness, isolation, and self-estrangement all exhibit strong negative and significant effects on efficacy. The effects of all individual measures of alienation on efficacy do not vary across prisons. The modern philosophy of prison management—a bridge between the keeper philosophy and strict order maintenance to ensure safety of inmates and workers—alienates prison workers in order to meet security goals and provide appropriate treatment of prisoners (DiIulio 1987; Lombardo 1989). But as these results indicate, alienated prison workers are less effective at prisoner management. It is conceded that the prison management shift in emphasis to control and custody was warranted. But the effects of increased formality (reduced discretion and informality) diminish the perceived efficacy of prison workers. Reducing the ability for prison workers to dictate outcomes and connect with their work environment has harmful effects on prisoner management. These are important and robust results that hold up across all years of analysis and suggest the salience of alienation on the perception of prisoner management.

Hypothesis 3b: *Well-supervised, treatment-oriented institutions will improve inmate management. Fearful institutions will aggravate inmate management.*

Counter to Hypothesis (3b), the current specified models are not able to fully explain the significant variation across institutions. Hypothesis (3b) posits that well-supervised and treatment-oriented facilities will improve individual efficacy. These institutional level variables do not prove to be significant across four years of analysis (Table 5.2). Aggregate levels of satisfaction with supervision and treatment-oriented prisons do not significantly impact efficacy. Alienation specifically diagrams the importance of social relationships within institutions (in this case, relationships with other prison workers, with supervisors, and with inmates). But at the institutional level, mean levels of these aggregated relationship variables do not impact individual efficacy (with one exception).

Notably, the aggregation of orientation—where high scores indicate a custodial perspective toward corrections—is significantly and negatively related to efficacy in year 2007 (Table 5.2). In line with Hypothesis (3b) this suggests that in one analysis year custody-oriented correctional institutions negatively impacted individual perceptions of inmate management. But this finding does not hold up across years and is therefore largely diminished by lack of ample support. In addition, fearful institutions do appear to contribute negatively to efficacy but only in year 2007 (Table 5.2). Again, the import of such a finding is largely reduced since it does not hold up across all four years. Even fully specified models continue to show significant variation at the institutional level. As specified, therefore, this indicates that the models do not fully explain the level-2 variance. Yet, when considered in relation to the total variance of the dependent variable explained by the fully specified models, this is a relatively small concern (see Chapter 7).

Table 5.2   Efficacy Regressed on Alienation (*HLM with REML and robust standard errors*)

	Model 2 (2007) Coefficient (Stand. Error)	Model 2 (2008) Coefficient (Stand. Error)	Model 2 (2009) Coefficient (Stand. Error)	Model 2 (2010) Coefficient (Stand. Error)
Institutional Level				
Intercept	−0.010	0.126***	0.015	0.006
	(0.014)	(0.019)	(0.014)	(0.014)
Supervision	−0.034	−0.005	0.035	0.041
	(0.038)	(0.086)	(0.046)	(0.051)
Orientation	−0.180**	−0.075	−0.045	0.049
	(0.065)	(0.086)	(0.075)	(0.067)
Fear	−0.078*	−0.070	−0.005	0.033
	(0.032)	(0.059)	(0.038)	(0.036)
Prison Age	0.000	−0.000	0.000	0.001
	(0.000)	(0.000)	(0.000)	(0.000)
Gender	−0.180	0.550	0.596**	0.199
	(0.065)	(0.295)	(0.216)	(0.202)
Race	0.069	0.035	0.259**	0.048
	(0.092)	(0.151)	(0.891)	(0.093)
High Security	−0.103	0.099	−0.215**	−0.278**
	(0.061)	(0.088)	(0.078)	(0.086)
Medium Security	−0.016	0.106	−0.028	−0.115*
	(0.047)	(0.066)	(0.051)	(0.055)
Low Security	0.063	0.171*	0.078	−0.013
	(0.053)	(0.076)	(0.050)	(0.053)
Minimum Security	0.096	0.095	0.059	−0.019
	(0.093)	(0.099)	(0.099)	(0.099)
Individual Level				
Alienation	−0.447***	−0.521***	−0.460***	−0.471***
	(0.014)	(0.022)	(0.018)	(0.015)
Race Black	0.090**	0.078	0.041	0.131**
	(0.033)	(0.051)	(0.047)	(0.038)
Female	−0.134***	−0.149**	−0.128**	−0.063*
	(0.033)	(0.045)	(0.040)	(0.031)
20+ Years at BOP	0.239***	0.063	0.058	0.050
	(0.049)	(0.042)	(0.054)	(0.036)
Inmate Contact	0.751***	0.812***	0.751***	0.702***
	(0.068)	(0.092)	(0.075)	(0.067)
High School	−0.096*	−0.021	−0.050	−0.076
	(0.040)	(0.048)	(0.038)	(0.039)
Line-Staff	−0.099**	−0.052	−0.132	−0.100**
	(0.031)	(0.045)	(0.038)	(0.030)
Variance Components	X^2	X^2	X^2	X^2
U_0	133.774*	146.282**	100.468	142.709**
$U_{Alienation}$	141.051*	158.175**	149.171*	139.273

Source: Data from the PSCS, Federal Bureau of Prisons, 2006–2010.
*p<0.05; **p<0.01; ***p<0.001.

Fully specified models also consider demographics (at the institutional level), geographical region, and security level. But the results are not conclusive and are largely restricted to single year analysis. For example, year 2008 suggests that low-security prisons exhibit a strong and positive impact on efficacy but year 2007 finds no effect of institutional security level on efficacy (Table 5.2). Moreover, years 2009 and 2010 suggest that high security prisons significantly and negatively impact efficacy (Table 5.2). It appears therefore that conclusions cannot be drawn regarding the effect of security level on the outcome of efficacy. Demographically, year 2009 finds positive and significant race (black) and gender (female) effects on efficacy. But these results are not supported in other years. It is unclear, therefore, if race and gender on the institutional level play a role in perception of effectiveness of inmate management on the individual level. Strong conclusions cannot be drawn about institutional level effects. Of course, it is important to note that the selected level-2 variables are not able to explain the entire variation. Yet, as Chapter 7 demonstrates, this is a relatively small concern. Nevertheless, Hypothesis (3b) is not supported by these results.

Hypothesis 3c: *The alienation impact on inmate management is greatest in high-security prisons.*

Hypothesis (3c) predicts that the impact of alienation on efficacy will be most pronounced in high-security prisons. Composition of the prisoner population, ratio of workers to inmates, and physical layouts characterize the key differences between security levels. Results indicate that high-security prisons do significantly increase the negative impact that alienation has on efficacy for years 2008 and 2009 but these results are not duplicated in 2010 and 2007 (Table 5.3). Yet, the results in 2008 and 2009 hold across individual level measures of alienation and at least warrant further discussion and future investigation.

Feeling powerless in a high-security facility is apparently more damaging to effective prisoner management than it is in other institutions. This finding is substantial in 2008 and 2009 but does not gain significance in 2007 and 2010 (Table 5.3). Meaninglessness in high-security prisons has an enhanced negative effect on efficacy in at least one year of analysis but again fails to reach significance in interaction in the remaining three years. Normlessness also appears to be more detrimental to efficacy in high-security prisons, at least for year 2009. Similarly, high-security prisons appear to increase the negative impact of isolation on efficacy and high-security prisons across three years (2007–2009) aggravate the negative impact of self-estrangement on efficacy. High-security prisons likely house more aggressive and antisocial populations and these populations likely exacerbate the negative impact of

Table 5.3 Efficacy Regressed on Alienation: Cross-Level Interactions (*HLM with REML and robust standard errors*)

	2007	2008	2009	2010
	Coefficient (S. E.)	Coefficient (S. E.)	Coefficient (S. E.)	Coefficient (S. E.)
Alienation*	—	−0.127**	−0.185****	—
High Security		(0.059)	(0.042)	
Powerlessness*	—	−0.119***	−0.141***	—
High Security		(0.037)	(0.042)	
Meaninglessness*	—	−0.134***	—	—
High Security		(0.045)		
Normlessness*	—	—	−0.168****	—
High Security			(0.040)	
Isolation*	—	—	−0.127**	—
High Security			(0.053)	
Self-Estrangement*	—	−0.097*	−0.098***	—
High Security		(0.055)	(0.035)	
Isolation*	—	−0.166*	—	−0.082*
Minimum Security		(0.094)		(0.049)

Source: Data from the PSCS, Federal Bureau of Prisons, 2006–2010.
*p<0.1; **p<0.05; ***p<0.01; ****p<0.001.

alienation on efficacy. Moreover, routines in high-security facilities arguably follow strict protocol that minimizes informal and spontaneous interaction and activity. Therefore, the level of alienation is potentially higher and the subsequent impact of that alienation is also more substantial in high-security institutions. Hypothesis (3c) is largely supported by these results.

In addition, findings suggest that minimum- and medium-security prisons may also have an impact on the effect of alienation measures (this was not strictly proposed by Hypothesis 3c). Results in 2008 and 2010 (Table 5.3) suggest that minimum-security prisons increase the negative effect of isolation on efficacy. Institutions with the fewest physical restrictions—that house less aggressive and less dangerous men and women—appear to further aggravate isolated individuals' ability to manage prisoners. Notably, results regarding minimum-security prisons and self-estrangement are unclear due to the changing sign of self-estrangement between 2007/2008 and 2010. Medium-security prisons in 2009 mitigate the negative impact of normlessness on efficacy. Results from 2009 also suggest medium-security prisons soften the negative impact of isolation on efficacy. The environment of medium-security prisons, therefore, appears to buffer negative effects of alienation on efficacy.

Results indicate that alienation negatively impacts the ability for prison workers to manage inmate populations. This finding supports Hypothesis (3a). Individual level processes appear to be more salient than institutional level processes (due to consistent significance across years). Hypothesis (3b) is not supported by this analysis. Unconditional models verify that institutional level variation is modest. But significant variation at the institutional level exists and continues to exist in fully specified models. Individual level variables do not fully explain variation at the institutional level (Model 1, not shown). But institutional level variables are not consistently found to be related to effectiveness in prisoner management (counter to Hypothesis [3b]). Aligned with Hypothesis (3c), high-security prisons are found to aggravate alienation's impact on efficacy. Medium-security and minimum-security prisons also appear to impact alienation's impact on efficacy. These results indicate that the institutional environment—potentially the composition of prisoners and the physical layout—influences the effect of alienation on prisoner management.

RESULTS: ALIENATION AND HARDENING

Hypothesis 4a: *Alienation hardens prison workers.*

Hypothesis (4a) predicts that alienation will emotionally harden prison workers. Results indicate that alienation is significantly and positively associated with emotional hardening across all four years of alienation (Table 5.4). This finding is replicated by individual measures of alienation as well as by the overall measure of alienation developed through principal component factor analysis. Years 2008–2010 also find that the effect of alienation varies across institutions—as indicated by significant variation in slope estimates across institutions (Table 5.4). Alienation (and its individual measures entered into individual models) increases mean levels of emotional hardening across institutions and the slope effect largely varies by institution. After considering only individual level variables, significant variation still exists across prisons and warrants additional multi-level analysis (not shown). Modern prison management promotes environments that alienate in order to better protect workers and prisoners. Results indicate that alienation hardens prison workers. The keeper philosophy lauds a perspective that demands: "the prisoner is not to suffer pains beyond the deprivation of liberty" (DiIulio 1987, 167). It may appear difficult to reconcile these results with this philosophy. Institutions that emotionally harden staff—and increase the perception that inmates are objects—remove the humanity implied by the keeper philosophy. However, if security is the primary focus then emotional hardening might benefit prison management and promote impartial, albeit cold, treatment.

On the individual level, Race Black has a consistently significant and negative effect on emotional hardening. This relationship is maintained across all four years. Gender Female (on the individual level) does not reach

Table 5.4 Hardening Regressed on Alienation *(HLM with REML and robust standard errors)*

	Model 2 (2007) Coefficient (Stand. Error)	Model 2 (2008) Coefficient (Stand. Error)	Model 2 (2009) Coefficient (Stand. Error)	Model 2 (2010) Coefficient (Stand. Error)
Institutional Level				
Intercept	0.000	−0.115***	0.011	−0.001
	(0.014)	(0.020)	(0.015)	(0.015)
Supervision	−0.080	−0.042	0.002	−0.017
	(0.058)	(0.599)	(0.066)	(0.045)
Orientation	0.046	0.016	−0.003	−0.097
	(0.077)	(0.087)	(0.073)	(0.094)
Fear	0.026	0.009	0.058	0.100*
	(0.044)	(0.039)	(0.040)	(0.042)
Prison Age	0.000	−0.001*	−0.001	0.000
	(0.000)	(0.000)	(0.000)	(0.000)
Gender	−0.014	0.163	−0.289	−0.301
	(0.246)	(0.305)	(0.232)	(0.230)
Race Black	−0.358**	−0.108	−0.083	−0.061
	(0.105)	(0.123)	(0.099)	(0.104)
High Security	0.085	0.106	0.113	0.203*
	(0.062)	(0.092)	(0.073)	(0.092)
Low Security	−0.121**	−0.036	−0.025	−0.029
	(0.062)	(0.053)	(0.050)	(0.051)
Individual Level				
Alienation	0.429***	0.448***	0.432***	0.433***
	(0.013)	(0.022)	(0.019)	(0.016)
Race Black	−0.390***	−0.388***	−0.406***	−0.315***
	(0.045)	(0.052)	(0.044)	(0.042)
Female	−0.019	0.048	−0.029	−0.035
	(0.026)	(0.041)	(0.039)	(0.029)
20+ Years at BOP	0.105	0.163***	0.089	0.172***
	(0.065)	(0.038)	(0.047)	(0.038)
Inmate Contact	0.146*	0.195*	0.178*	0.103
	(0.060)	(0.077)	(0.071)	(0.059)
High School	−0.089*	−0.080	−0.075	−0.015
	(0.039)	(0.054)	(0.047)	(0.042)
Line-Staff	−0.226***	−0.146**[1]	−0.207***	−0.202***
	(0.028)	(0.041)	(0.044)	(0.031)
Variance Components	X^2	X^2	X^2	X^2
U_0	136.375**	124.989	106.126	154.829**
$U_{Alienation}$	107.334	150.270*	140.233*	154.717**

Source: Data from the PSCS, Federal Bureau of Prisons, 2006–2010.
*p<0.1; **p<0.05; ***p<0.01.

significance and flips signs through the years, providing little insight as to the impact of being female on emotional hardening. Prison workers with 20+ years of experience are more likely to be emotionally hardened. This relationship is significant for two years (2008 and 2010, Table 5.4) and is positively associated across all four years. High school education appears to protect against emotional hardening as it consistently exhibits a negative relationship (although this only reaches significance for year 2007, Table 5.4). Line-staff also appears to protect against emotional hardening and this significant finding is maintained across all four years and is rather robust. Taken together, prolonged exposure to prison environments appears to aggravate emotional hardening. However, lower education, race black, and line-staff appear to counter the impacts of emotional hardening.

Hypothesis 4b: *Institutions with lower perception of supervision, with stronger custodial orientations, and with greater fear of inmate populations harden prison workers.*

Results also indicate that institutional level variables of interest (Hypothesis [4b])—specifically, aggregations of perception of supervision and custodial orientation—do not have an effect on emotional hardening on the individual level. Due to changing signs of orientation and supervision across years, meaningful conclusions cannot be drawn about the direction of these level-2 variables in relation to emotional hardening. Institutional fear is positively associated with emotional hardening and reaches significance in year 2010 (Table 5.4), but fails to reach significance in other years. Primary institutional level variables are not significant in this analysis. Support is not found for Hypothesis (4b). On the institutional level, increases in percent black and percent female appear to protect individuals from emotional hardening but these fail to gain significance except for the year 2007 and only for race black (not shown). High-security prisons appear to aggravate emotional hardening. Again this only reaches significance for one year (not shown). Low-security prisons also maintain a consistently negative relationship with emotional hardening and gain significance in 2007 (not shown).

Hypothesis 4c: *Alienation in high-security prisons enhances hardening of prison workers. Alienation in minimum-security prisons will decrease hardening.*

Hypothesis (4c) posits that alienation in high-security prisons will enhance emotional hardening of prison workers, and alienation in minimum-security prisons will diminish emotional hardening. Results indicate that neither position is supported for the overall alienation measure. However minimum-security prisons appear to operate as a protective factor in 2007 and 2008 (not shown), particularly for those who rank high in the measure of meaninglessness (this is not confirmed by results in 2009 and 2010). Mixed results appear regarding isolation and minimum security. In 2007, minimum-security facilities appear to act as an aggravator and in 2008 they appear to act as a protective factor. Years 2009 and 2010 do not confirm either of these findings. For prison workers who are particularly self-estranged, jail appears to lessen the impact this estrangement has on emotional hardening. This result is found in 2007 and in 2010. Depending on the type of alienation, security level may either buffer or aggravate the negative effect alienation has on emotional hardening. In certain years, the negative impact of specific measures of alienation appears to be buffered by security level. This suggests that prisoner composition and physical layout may mitigate (or aggravate) alienation effects. Hypothesis (4c) is partly supported if alienation as meaninglessness is considered.

Taken together, alienation positively and significantly impacts emotional hardening. This result is robust and significance is reached across all four years of analysis. This supports Hypothesis (4a). In the case of emotional hardening, individual level processes appear to be more salient than institutional-level processes (due to consistent significance across years). Hypothesis (4b) is not supported by analysis. Institutional level variables exhibit minimal impact on individual outcome of emotional hardening. But significant variation at the institutional level exists and continues to exist in specified models. Individual level variables do not fully explain variation at the institutional level (not shown). Only equivocal conclusions may be drawn about cross-level interactions. Current analysis finds partial support for Hypothesis (4c)—but only if meaninglessness is adopted as the alienation measure. Emotional hardening may be best understood as an individual process that is not dependent on security level but is highly related to level of alienation.

SUMMARY OF RESULTS: ALIENATION IN PRISONS

Results indicate that efficacy is not only influenced by power adoptions but that it is also influenced by alienation. Prison workers who report advanced levels of alienation perceive less ability to manage inmate populations. Institutional level variables—that specifically capture affairs between workers, supervisors, and prisoners—do not appear to be consistently salient in this relationship. Modern approaches to prison management are naturally designed to alienate workers. This alienation harms prison oversight in multiple ways. Not only does alienation directly impact effectiveness in management but it also hardens prison workers. Findings suggest that both outcomes are avoidable and unnecessary.

All five types of alienation are robust predictors of efficacy and emotional hardening. Indeed, alienation is particularly powerful in explaining the variation across both of these dependent variables. By definition, alienation is an individual's perception of the social climate. It is not contradictory or problematic to propose that individual perception may be felt uniquely—or in isolation—by a large collection of individuals and that this collective perception is detrimental to prison management. In this instance, however, collective perception does not have a unifying factor that publicly connects the population of individuals (that would extinguish the perception of alienation). Nevertheless, singular processes appear to drive the alienation of individual members. This study divides alienation into five categories: powerlessness, meaninglessness, normlessness, isolation, and self-estrangement. Each of these five categories is particularly salient in the prediction of efficacy and emotional hardening. Reductions in these categories are likely to improve outcomes in prisoner management and are much easier to grasp from a practical or policy perspective.

Increasing discretion and injecting meaning and collectivity into prison work may help to alleviate alienation and may be a logical place to begin. Without external respect and acknowledgment that prison workers assume roles that the public demands, prison workers may have difficulty finding meaning in their work (accolades from prisoners are unlikely). It may be possible to increase discretion by including line-staff in decision-making processes—no matter how insignificant (Aiken and Hage 1966). It may also be possible to generate communal norms by increasing solidarity among workers and by promoting policies that reflect collective responsibility over self-survival. It is perhaps unsurprising that high-security prisons appear to increase the negative impact of alienation on efficacy (this relationship reaches significance across two years). Strict protocols and rigid population oversight are probably not negotiable in high-security settings.

It is important to stress that alienation increases the emotional hardening of the prison worker. Alienation increases the likelihood that prison workers perceive their charges as objects and increases prison worker irritability and emotional exhaustion. The eventual release of over 90% of all prisoners (Petersilia 2003)—coupled with a 67% recidivism rate (Langan and Levin 2002)—suggests that what happens in prison is not helping prisoners. This does not suggest that prison is criminogenic. Institutions that harden workers are likely to negatively impact charges.

Coupled with reduced efficacy, it appears that alienation is responsible for unfavorable outcomes within the prison environment. The dual impact of alienation on prison workers could dramatically reduce the effectiveness of programming implementation of innovative strategies that aim to reduce recidivism rates. It is an overlooked reality that reentry needs to begin in prisons and that prison workers must subscribe to rehabilitation programming in order for these programs to find success. Prison workers who believe that they are able to handle inmates and who see those inmates as people are arguably more advantageous to treatment.

Chapter 6

Prison Theory

The aim of this chapter is to develop the foundation for a criminal justice theory that revolves around prison management and illustrates the potentially malleable nature of the prison worker experience. This chapter employs the framework and premises generated in the previous chapters. Previous chapters provide much greater depth and discussion of prison management, power, and alienation.

GENERAL THEORETICAL PROPOSAL

Prison impacts prisoners *and* prison workers. The Bureau of Prisons employs over 38,000 men and women to supervise the inmate population (Samuels 2014) of about 217,000 people (USDOJ 2014). In a sense, these are total institutions (Goffman 1961). I argue that current corrections literature could be substantially improved by developing a criminal justice theory of prison institutions that focuses on prison management and prison workers. I propose a foundation for criminal justice theory that draws on prison management philosophy and is tested by an analysis of prison workers. Current management perspectives arguably adopt necessary perspectives on security and order maintenance but these perspectives are not without consequences. Critically, extant literature largely neglects to consider prison management philosophy and therefore fails to consider the inevitable alienation of prison workers. I contend that studies that pursue outcomes such as job satisfaction, turnover, absenteeism, and role ambiguity, for example, only target the *symptoms* of alienation. Therefore, I reason that these studies are incomplete. Advancing a theory of prison institutions that understands the high likelihood of alienation will serve to further understand the nature of coercive institutions and therefore the impact of lengthy exposure to such institutions.

Prison administrators are limited by the variety of power that they may employ. This restriction permits simple evaluation of malleable management strategies. Ultimately, empowering workers is possible without undermining security efforts. Using survey data from the Federal Bureau of Prisons, this chapter furthers two related propositions: (1) constructive and positive power adoptions can reduce prison worker alienation and (2) a criminal justice theory of prisons is integral to understanding the impact of prison on prisoners and prison workers. Without advancing theoretical propositions on the nature of incarceration, we are left with an inevitable but ineffective place that is the modern prison.

PRISON MANAGEMENT

DiIulio's (1987) prison management platform promotes order, amenity, and service. He endorses consistency and rationality in prison management and suggests that central authorities and paramilitary structure will generate ordered, serene, and safe prisons (DiIulio 1987, 256). Indeed, according to DiIulio (1987) safe and humane prison environments hail from strong order. Perhaps most importantly, security must be the priority for management. In strict opposition to sociological dogma and later aided in part by important prison riot literature (Useem and Kimball 1989; see also Useem and Piehl 2006), DiIulio (1987) convincingly portrays mismanagement and not management per se as conducive to violent and lethal outcomes within prison institutions.

But the preservation of order in theory and in practice may diverge. Prisoner oversight in practice is complex. Even though general prison management perspectives explicitly accept that detention is sufficient punishment and that physical and sexual assaults within prisons cannot be tolerated (DiIulio 1987; Jurik and Musheno 1986; Bureau of Prisons 2011), correctional officers are asked to oversee antisocial populations that have largely expressed little concern for the social order and to do so without bias and without emotion. Although these populations of men and women may terrify the public (DiIulio 1987, 169), inhumane treatment of these populations technically violates the "keeper" philosophy. This is one indication that emotional dissociation is potentially advantageous to humane prisoner treatment. Perhaps even more importantly, this denial of torture must be met because prisons are only legitimate insofar as they protect prisoners and prison workers (and fairly and consistently supervise staff and charges alike).

CORRECTIONAL BASES OF POWER AND ALIENATION

Hepburn (1985) defines five "bases of power" that prison workers may employ in prison institutions. Instead of defining power adoptions from the perspective of prisoners, this chapter endorses a position that asks prison workers to define power via their perception of the prison administration and their perception of supervision. Power therefore arrives by way of management and therefore can be controlled or altered through directives.

Power shapes prison environments. And current management philosophies arguably alienate prison workers. At one level, prisons are constructed to capably detain men and women who possess irrepressible antisocial inclinations. The utility of prisons is therefore practical and moral. Practical confinement for those who will not reject impulse and moral confinement to supervise these unruly populations without judgment. The systematic torture of inmates would certainly qualify as irresponsible and would largely be rejected by constitutional challenge. But the moral demand for humane treatment of prisoners also invests in a practical component of prison workers' well-being. Indeed, the "keeper" philosophy—the loss of liberty is adequate punishment—does not simply protect the prisoners but it also encourages emotional distance.

Although the detached relationship between overseer and charge may be necessary to ensure humane and safe prisons, it may not be beneficial for the same relationship to exist between line-staff and supervisors. The reduction in personal contact by overseers may be a direct consequence of security-focused institutions (but transmission of institutional activity and knowledge from inmates to correctional officers surely helps to predict violence). Therefore, with security as a priority it may be inappropriate to ask the prison worker to derive worth and meaning from her work through direct prisoner oversight. It may be preferable to ask that she derive worth from the institution and the administration. It is conceded that alienation is an ambiguous idea that often evokes industrialization and the conversion of human muscle to machine. But I reason that alienation is centrally concerned with individual self-worth and originates from the collective.

THE CURRENT INQUIRY

The aim of the current inquiry is to develop the foundation for criminal justice theory that revolves around prison management and illustrates the malleable nature of the prison worker experience. I contend that power can either reduce or aggravate worker alienation. Power adoptions that reduce alienation serve as constructive tools for prison administrators and will benefit the institution at large. Due to a strict security and order maintenance focus (DiIulio 1987), I also have proposed that modern prisons endorse—explicitly and implicitly—alienation practices. Prison administrators have few options relative to power employment. But I contend that a stringent concentration on empowerment will assuage the institutional tendency toward alienation of its workers. I test two specific and related hypotheses: (1) legitimate, expert, and referent power strategies will reduce alienation among prison workers and (2) coercive and reward power strategies will increase alienation among prison workers.

The aim of this study is not only to determine that coercive institutions have necessary consequences but also to illustrate that policies and practices within the facility—tools that do not contradict the goals of security—are available to reduce the impact of these consequences. Understanding the prison institution in this lens will help to generate programming that is suitable and reflective of the coercive environment. This perspective highlights what is needed to secure the safety of prisoners and prison workers while also highlighting areas that may be adjusted and manipulated in order to improve the worker experience. Reflective of DiIulio (1987), I suggest that prison administrators control prisons and therefore prison workers are at the heart of a criminal justice theory of prisons. First, it is vital to understand the environment we have constructed to detain those who are unwilling or unable to abide by the general will. After this conceptualization, it is appropriate to configure, within those confines, constructive and effective programming to support those detained.

DATA AND MEASURES

This study draws on data from the Federal Bureau of Prisons yearly Prison Social Climate Survey (PSCS). This study uses responses from calendar year 2010 ($n = 10,058$). In calendar year 2010, four versions of the PSCS are distributed to sampled populations. Since variable construction largely relies on two of these versions, a notable decrease in the sampled population inevitably occurs. Notably, prison workers are randomly selected from within demographic categories and survey versions are also randomly selected for the individual.

The alienation measures employ theoretical constructs first specified by Seeman (1959). Although prior research has used these constructs to evaluate prison workers (Poole and Regoli 1981), prior research has not used federal prison workers as its target population and has not incorporated these constructs in a test of a theory of prison effects. Through principal component factor analysis, I compose five alienation measures: powerlessness, normlessness, meaninglessness, isolation, and self-estrangement (see Chapter 5).

I also construct a single measure that is generated out of these five variables. The overall import, thereby, is the realization of a singular latent quality that is only grasped in its parts (i.e., via five entangled conceptualizations). I have created, in this way, a single dependent variable that is only understood through five complementary observations. From a policy perspective, this is advantageous as it helps to illuminate how specifically administrators may improve management and oversight of worker populations.

Reflecting Hepburn (1985), I contend that prison workers are able to control prison environments through five power strategies (see Chapter 4). Proxies are developed for each of these power adoptions (see Table 5.1). Research to date has not tested the impact of power adoptions on alienation measures. I argue that prison administrators are able to formally condone and effectively supervise to ensure the adoption of specific power strategies among prison workers. Unlike the analysis in Chapter 4, I conceptualize legitimacy through fair treatment. Prison workers who perceive that they are treated fairly will also perceive that the system, indeed the prison itself, is legitimate (see Sherman 1993). Remaining power conceptualizations are reflective of the analysis in Chapter 4.

General demographics are also considered in this analysis in order to ensure that individual characteristics of prison workers are not largely responsible for alienation outcomes. Divergence in attitude toward prisoners does exist in the literature (Britton 1997; Cullen et al. 1989; Jackson and Ammen 1996; Jurik 1985), although Whitehead and Lindquist (1989) suggest this phenomenon is largely due to organizational factors. But due to power dynamics within prison it is important to note the race and gender effects on alienation outcomes as they may dictate organizational climate. In addition, years spent working in the Bureau of Prisons is used as opposed to age since increased exposure to the prison environment is considered to be more relevant to alienation rather than simple age irrespective of exposure (see Chapter 4).

RESULTS

Before analyzing the effect of power adoptions on alienation among prison workers, I first construct a series of dependent and independent measures through principal component factor analysis. Results indicate that constructed measures are appropriate for analysis (see Table 5.1). Although alpha scores for select variables are somewhat low, all constructed measures sufficiently load onto a single factor and therefore suggest a single latent variable. Thus, dependent and independent measures appear to share a great deal of similarity with the underlying trait. It is deliberate that power measures and alienation measures are strictly reflective of experiences with supervisors and the prison institution and governing body as a whole. These factors are considered to be malleable without severe undermining of the goals of prison safety.

Hypothesis 1 posits that legitimate, expert, and referent power strategies will reduce alienation among prison workers. Results from linear regression with robust standard errors reveal that constructive power strategies correspond to reductions in alienation (Table 6.1). Specifically, legitimate, expert, and referent power significantly and negatively predict isolation, powerlessness, meaninglessness, normlessness, and self-estrangement. This consistent and robust finding across outcomes suggests that federal institutions are able to manipulate alienation measures by adopting positive power strategies that essentially empower workers. Said differently, if management respects, trains, and treats fairly their workers it is more likely that they will be able to combat the necessary alienation of prison institutions.

Hypothesis 2 posits that coercive and reward power adoptions will increase alienation. Results suggest a more nuanced finding here. Coercive power appears to be positively related to alienation within the prison institution. Notably, coercive power appears to positively correspond to isolation, powerlessness, and normlessness. This suggests that intimidation may isolate the prison worker, make him perceive that he cannot shape outcomes, and increase the murkiness of appropriate oversight within the confines of detention centers. However, unlike the prediction of Hypothesis 2, reward power negatively corresponds to powerlessness, meaninglessness, normlessness, and self-estrangement. Due to the limitations of the reward measure (restricted by one response), it may be advantageous to verify this finding. However, if confirmed, it is possible that the prison worker perceives pay and performance to be explicitly and implicitly entangled. But the precise inference here is unclear. It is important to remember that these are human-service environments. Therefore, informal interactions are inevitable and the perception of officially unsanctioned raises may be erroneous in practice but considered common in institutional lore. Officers who subscribe to this perception may attempt to gain favor among supervisors and consequently strictly adhere to institutional norms and accept institutional code and culture. Note, however, that reward power is complemented by legitimate, expert, and referent power—all of which appear to have a more robust relationship with alienation measures.

Demographically, gender appears to play a small role. Being female appears to protect against self-estrangement. This may be due to the type of woman who selects prison work as an occupation. Race Black appears to protect against isolation and against normlessness. Results suggest that line-staff are protected by normlessness but are at particular risk for meaninglessness and self-estrangement. This is perhaps unsurprising. The work may have little value and little importance beyond survival, but the rules are understood.

Table 6.1 Alienation Regressed on Power Adoptions (OLS with robust standard errors)

	Isolation	Powerlessness	Meaninglessness	Normlessness	Self–Estrng
	Coefficient (S. E)	Coefficient (S. E)	Coefficient (S. E)	Coefficient (S. E)	Coefficient (S. E)
Intercept	0.0025	−0.0432*	−0.0090	0.0452*	−0.0257
	(0.024)	(0.020)	(0.017)	(0.017)	(0.022)
Independent Measures					
Legitimate Power	−0.1078***	−0.0889***	−0.2627***	−0.2556***	−0.1139***
	(0.023)	(0.018)	(0.018)	(0.018)	(0.023)
Expert Power	−0.2542***	−0.2759***	−0.3053***	−0.2874***	−0.0288***
	(0.018)	(0.014)	(0.013)	(0.013)	(0.018)
Referent Power	−0.1446***	−0.3235***	−0.1757***	−0.2973***	−0.1703**
	(0.023)	(0.018)	(0.017)	(0.017)	(0.023)
Coercive Power	0.0206*	0.0461**	0.006	0.0744***	0.0100
	(0.017)	(0.0135)	(0.012)	(0.012)	(0.017)
Reward Power	−0.0648	−0.1023***	−0.2036***	−0.0427**	−0.0694***
	(0.017)	(0.0150)	(0.013)	(0.013)	(0.016)
Demographic Controls					
Female	0.0529	0.1137	−0.0324	0.0236	−0.0630*
	(0.029)	(0.025)	(0.022)	(0.022)	(0.028)
Race Black	−0.1201**	−0.0381	−0.0301	−0.163***	−0.0102
	(0.035)	(0.026)	(0.026)	(0.027)	(0.034)
Line-Staff	0.0494	0.1092	0.0787**	−0.0941***	0.2341***
	(0.033)	(0.0267)	(0.023)	(0.024)	(0.031)
20+ Years	−0.0414	−0.0661	−0.0112	0.0124	−0.0680*
	(0.029)	(0.024)	(0.021)	(0.021)	(0.022)
Variance Explained	22.45%	45.09%	57.59%	56.67%	31.14%

Source: Data from the PSCS, Federal Bureau of Prisons, 2010.
*p<0.05; **p<0.01; ***p<0.001.

Reflective of Toch and Klofas (1982), longer tenured prison workers are less self-estranged. Due to attrition, workers who continue to pursue correctional work presumably have gained some value in it.

The variance of the outcomes explained by the regression models is substantial and appears to suggest that power adoptions are critical in the reduction of alienation among prison workers (Table 6.1). Power models explain 22% of the isolation outcome, 45% of the powerlessness outcome, 57% of the meaninglessness outcome, 56% of the normlessness outcome, and 31% of the self-estrangement outcome. These results do not suggest that the Bureau of Prisons should transform their management philosophy, instead they serve to illustrate the theoretical importance of power and alienation within the coercive environment.

DISSOCIATION, EXHAUSTION, AND COMMITMENT

In order to employ legitimate power and to increase perceived—and therefore objective—fairness, correctional officers arguably benefit from personal distance from prisoners. This is not to suggest that prison workers should treat prisoners as physical objects. Rather, security requires a nuanced approach and security focuses may generate specific types of environments. Certain types of officers with certain qualities may be beneficial to the goals of security. Prisons are not like other institutions in this regard. Prison workers cannot sanction verbal assaults nor can researchers deny their existence. Acknowledging that prisoners are often antisocial (by definition) also acknowledges that prisoners may act unruly, disrespectful. Navigating an environment of this nature may require a level of dissociation. This does not preclude the keeper philosophy from ensuring that prison itself—deprivation of liberty—is the punishment. But it does not follow that depersonalization promotes or even leads to inhumane treatment.

In addition, physical and emotional exhaustion are likely directly related to alienation. I constructed an alienation measure (by combing all five generated alienation measures through principal component factoring analysis), which strongly predicts emotional and physical exhaustion.[1] Prison administrators are better suited, I argue, to target alienation through power adoptions rather than attempt to understand how to limit specified burnout measures. I further contend that the appropriate way to manage this incredibly complex environment is to employ readily available tools. Constructive power strategies appear to reduce alienation, which subsumes the intent of burnout and predicts emotional and physical exhaustion.

Of course, implicit in this discussion is the role of attrition and job satisfaction. Without direct acknowledgment, correctional officer literature is largely and indirectly addressing alienation through its symptoms. Research suggests that prison itself may improve its ability to keep personnel. Strong organizational commitment appears to be negatively related to absenteeism (Lambert et al. 2005) and staff turnover (Mitchell et al. 2000; Camp 1994). Perhaps due to its potential link to turnover (and its resulting institutional costs), there has been considerable focus on correctional officer stress (Dowden and Tellier 2004). And while turnover rates can be as high as 38% (Schaufeli and Peeters 2000), generally the new and inexperienced quit. Organizational commitment, moreover, may be bolstered by increases in perception of discretionary ability—or the ability to shape outcomes (see Dowden and Tellier 2004). This increase in decision-making may improve job satisfaction (Lambert, Hogan, and Barton 2002). Essentially, injecting voice or power into the officer—reducing *powerlessness*—may improve commitment and turnover. Moreover, preliminary analysis presented here shows that alienation significantly reduces institutional commitment (Table 6.2).

Several limitations to this study are worth mentioning. Dependent and independent variables were constructed through principal component factor analysis. The selection of the components was based on agreement with theoretical arguments. It is likely that the selected and final constructs are not the only possible configuration to obtain latent variables. In addition, data for this study were obtained through the Bureau of Prisons and may not reflect practices or conditions in state prisons or in local jails. The analysis is also a cross-sectional examination for calendar year 2010. Future research should address the

Table 6.2 Exhaustion and Commitment Regressed on Alienation *(OLS with robust standard errors)*

	Exhaustion	Institutional Commitment
	Coefficient (S. E.)	*Coefficient (S. E.)*
Intercept	0.0361	0.0606
	(0.025)	(0.0541)
Alienation	0.4674**	−0.5498**
	(0.015)	(0.014)
Female	0.030	−0.0309
	(0.030)	(0.029)
Race Black	−0.1102*	−0.2684**
	(0.037)	(0.034)
Line-Staff	−0.2490**	0.2286**
	(0.032)	(0.029)
20+ Years BOP	0.1861**	0.0232
	(0.030)	(0.029)
Inmate Contact	0.0257	−0.0861
	(0.064)	(0.054)

Source: Data from the PSCS, Federal Bureau of Prisons, 2010.
*p<0.05; **p<0.001.

salience of the results found here and see if they are replicated in other coercive centers and whether or not they hold up across years of analysis. Since this is a cross-sectional analysis, the establishment of causality is not possible. However, the robust findings in this analysis do warrant serious consideration for the advancement of prison theory—a central concern of this inquiry.

PRISON THEORY

The composition of the alienation measure is particularly helpful for the prison environment because it allows for a variety of ways for management to address prison workers and improve commitment, reduce exhaustion, increase communication, and ensure consistent and systematic rule adherence. Farkas (1999) notes that the most satisfying aspect of correctional work may be related to pay and benefits and not to direct work with inmates. Although overseeing human actors, theoretical arguments must take this into consideration: prison work meaning may have little to do with prisoners. Prison workers may derive meaning from pay, and job satisfaction may reflect their experience with their union (see Page 2011). However, communication and rule adherence are vital qualities to ensure safe prisons (Useem and Kimball 1989). Reducing alienation likely improves security.

The theoretical framework presented here suggests that alienation is a central consequence to effective prison management. But the negative effects of alienation, I have argued, can be mitigated by carefully selecting constructive power adoptions. Prisons revolve around power and power adoptions are a concrete tool available to prison managers. Preliminary results suggest that careful consideration of power within the prison institution will benefit a variety of outcomes from exhaustion to job satisfaction. I propose that the central outcomes of concern for prison worker literature are reflective of the necessary yet troubling concept of alienation. Alienation may be necessary but it must be addressed proactively in order to ensure that it is limited, restricted, and contained.

NOTE

1. Exhaustion is a self-reported measure that averages 7-point Likert responses (all the time, very often, often, now and then, rarely, very rarely, never) to three survey questions: (1) A feeling of being emotionally drained at the end of the day; (2) A feeling that working with people all day is really a strain for you; and (3) A feeling of being fatigued when you get up in the morning and have to face another day on the job (Prison Social Climate Survey, Federal Bureau of Prisons, 2010).

Chapter 7

Conclusion

Failed policies largely generated by the New Penology doctrine (DiIulio 1991b; Marquart and Roebuck 1985)—combined with assumptions in the ineffectiveness of rehabilitation and escalating crime rates (MacKenzie 2006)—transformed prison management. In the 1980s, security became the primary focus. The new evolution of management increased professionalism and formality (see Lombardo 1989). This approach, lauded by DiIulio (1987), promoted a strong central authority and strict adherence to officially sanctioned power strategies that targeted order maintenance. Riots and prison violence were blamed on inadequate, informal, and even careless management oversight (Useem and Kimball 1989)—not on the nature of imprisonment. New management strategies sought to correct these management failures and inadequacies. Indeed, the changes in management practices arguably oversaw substantial increase in order and reduction in chaos (Useem and Piehl 2006; Useem and Kimball 1989; see also Carroll 1998). This was beneficial progression.

I have advocated that the physical protection of prison workers and of prisoners is critical. But security perspectives cannot needlessly or irrationally trump all other services within the prison. Prison institutions that provide better protection of workers and prisoners understand the fluid nature of human relationships and human oversight. In this regard, amenity and service are integral to institutional stability (DiIulio 1987). They improve internal relationships, ameliorate forced detainment, and enhance security measures. Indeed, relationships are essential to prison management (Liebling 2004). And for good reason, much of the extant research targets the prisoner–staff relationship. If amenity and service ease chaos, then this is logical. Diverse prison populations have diverse needs. Prisons that improve access to a variety of needed services are likely to pacify discord. Access—to edible meals, to educational and vocational advancement, to mental health professionals, to exercise equipment, and to television—then improves stability and reduces chaos. I do not believe that access de-emphasizes security. Instead, I believe that access elevates security and acknowledges that prison itself does not advance civility but imprisonment practices can.

While I do not discount the value of the relationships between prisoners and prison workers, I have reasoned that the relationship between prison workers and prison managers (or the prison administration itself) is the fundamental relationship in prison management. If prison is to have any intention at all, then prison workers are to make the prison environment. Therefore, actual power assumptions of prison workers—as perceived through their institution of employment—are a notable empirical gap. Prison worker perception of internally promoted power strategies helps to understand limitations and realities of the prison administration. If prison workers perceive that prisons themselves promote and demand formal and constructive power strategies, then official decree is suitable for dictating culture. In essence, a central question of this book asks, in part, if informal and formal ethos complement one another in federal prisons. The results presented here suggest that they do— constructive power strategies appear to be favored (of course, these findings need to be replicated in state institutions).

In addition, civil discourse between prisoner and prison worker may be advantageous and even necessary. But I maintain that the prisoner does not define morality within the institution (see Bottoms and Tankebe 2012; Sparks and Bottoms 1995). Appropriately defined morality for prison practices reflects the greater social order. Balance (or peaceful interaction) achieved on housing units is not to be obtained through forfeiture of greater societal demands. A prison worker may learn how to manage prisoners through direct exposure but she learns right from wrong—institutional morality—from the culture of prison workers. A strong administration mandates that this culture reflects external social prescriptions of acceptable behavior. If prisons are to succeed, thereby, I further infer that there must be a logical intention and an unbreakable moral directive for acceptable and unacceptable treatment. The intention and the moral directive must be known and clearly designated. The keeper perspective strives to ensure that loss of liberty is sufficient punishment. This is an ideal, and unclear definitions of fair treatment make this ideal problematic, even (potentially) contradictory. But this is a compulsory foundation of prison management that must complement security goals. A strict security focus does not necessarily require adherence to the keeper philosophy. Instead, it may promote whatever tactics secure the facility. Prisons violate keeper mandates if prisoners are tortured *in any way*. But torture is bad management. And prisons are a manageable institution. Security measures that torture are therefore bad security measures.

But even nuanced and progressive security perspectives breed unwelcome consequences. In general, overall security depends on adherence to formal edict. Rulebooks that do not permit flexibility in oversight but demand accountability from individual workers may generate a series of problems. Official decrees trump informal relationships and accountability to management begins to revolve around adherence to those official decrees (Lombardo 1989). Evading blame for security lapses becomes vital and reduces commitment to peers. In fact, enhanced emotional separation of the prison worker from his peers, from his supervisors, and from prisoners may be inevitable (see Lombardo 1989). But I have largely contended that this reality is especially problematic in an institution that does not appropriately prioritize the relationship between prison workers and prison managers. Without appropriate prioritization, worker alienation from her employer, her peers, and her charges is likely. Through negligence or through keen awareness, the prison administration defines morality and culture. Messaging and presentation reflect loyalty or mistrust. In an ideal institution, the prison administration identifies with the prison worker and does not undermine her value. By definition, this solidarity does not shield workers who are immoral. Instead, it empowers workers to meet the morality of the institution (as derived from the social order). Workers, in this sense, do not hide behind a wall of silence and insulate peers from outside prosecution. Workers are an extension of the external justice system and symbolize fair treatment—embody morality.

The world inside prisons may change. There is consensus: we incarcerate too many men and women in the United States and decarceration strategies are necessary (see National Research Council 2014). Changes in imprisonment practices are possible, even likely. But since those we are afraid of will be the ones imprisoned, security cannot be limited or minimized. I reason that *rational* security measures must remain as the focal point of prison management. This requires prison rules that are logical, understandable, and transparent. This also means uniform rule enforcement. I find it troubling that complete rule enforcement is at times considered impossible, inappropriate, or even naïve within prison institutions (see, e.g., Liebling 2004, 2011). The suggestion that complete rule enforcement is impossible makes the prison institution itself impossible. To be clear, I believe that worker discretion is critical to management. But the real question is not how to blindly enforce all the rules but how to permit departures from the rules *within* the rules. Formal edict must lead. But this does not mandate an invalid flexibility or discretion. Written justifications for departures from official decree are a logical solution. This allows for cultural awareness of acceptable rationale for rule departure. I do not pretend that rulebooks themselves are sufficient as designed. But that is a fault in the institutional codes and not in the rules per se. Imperfect rule enforcement breeds bias and favoritism and dismantles the formal power structure. Consistent rule enforcement is predictable and—with the added possibility of departures due to contextual variation—fair.

As I have demonstrated, power and alienation are the integral phenomena in prison institutions. Until this work, research had neither explicitly evaluated the effects of alienation on prisoner management nor evaluated the perceived power strategies promoted by the prison institution. In order to produce an intentional prison, productive and humane culture and morality must be generated and enforced by the prison administration *through* the prison workers. Intentional prisons prioritize prison workers.

DETAILED SUMMARY OF RESULTS

Using data from the Federal Bureau of Prisons yearly Prison Social Climate Survey, I evaluated the perceived power strategies promoted by prison institutions (and its effects) and the impact of alienation on prisoner management. I then developed the basis for a criminal justice theory of prisons. My chief findings are:

- Formal and constructive power adoptions correspond to higher levels of institutional commitment. Elevated levels of institutional fear relate to reduced institutional commitment. The effect of legitimate power on commitment is reduced in jails.
- Formal and constructive power adoptions correspond to better prison management (coercive power also corresponds to better prison management). The effect of legitimate power on efficacy is increased in high-security institutions.
- Alienation corresponds to poor prisoner management. High-security prisons increase the negative impact that alienation has on efficacy.
- Alienation significantly and positively predicts emotional hardening of prison workers.
- Formal and constructive power strategies correspond to reduced alienation.

Consistent and significant results across four years suggest that individual level processes are vital to institutional and prisoner management. Comparison with unconditional models suggests that specified models explain a substantial proportion of the variances of the dependent variables. In addition, the introduction of only level-1 variables (Model 1) reduces the institutional level variances by a substantial amount. This further suggests that individual level variables are particularly salient in the prediction of the key outcomes. Discussion and further interpretation of the complete results ensue in the subsequent paragraphs and sections.

Tables 7.1, 7.2, and 7.3 summarize the main results by hypothesis and report the variance explained by each fully constructed model (MODEL 2). Individual level factors are highly significant across all four years and explain a substantial amount of variance across those years. As is shown in Table 7.1, all three positive and constructive power adoptions are significant in the predicted direction across all four years for the outcomes institutional commitment and efficacy. At the institutional level, fear plays an important role in predicting commitment. It is also clear that cross-level interactions do not reach significance across all four years (but legitimacy in high-security

Table 7.1   Results Summarized for Hypotheses 1 and 2

	2007	*2008*	*2009*	*2010*
Hypothesis 1				
Individual Level				
Legitimate (+)	✓	✓	✓	✓
Referent (+)	✓	✓	✓	✓
Expert (+)	✓	✓	✓	✓
Coercive (−)	−	✓	−	−
Reward (−)	−	−	−	x
Institutional Level				
Well-Super (+)	−	−	−	−
Treatment (+)	−	−	−	−
Fear (−)	✓	✓	✓	✓
Interactions				
Legit•High (+)	−	−	−	−
Rewrd•Min(+)	−	−	−	−
Refrnt•Min (+)	−	−	−	−
Hypothesis 2				
Individual Level				
Legitimate (+)	✓	✓	✓	✓
Referent (+)	✓	✓	✓	✓
Expert (+)	✓	✓	✓	✓
Coercive (−)	x	x	x	x
Reward (−)	−	−	✓	−
Institutional Level				
Well-Super (+)	−	−	−	−
Treatment (+)	✓	−	−	−
Fear (−)	−	−	−	−
Interactions				
Legit•High (+)	−	✓	✓	−
Exprt•High (+)	−	−	−	−
Rewrd•Min (+)	−	−	−	−
Refrnt•Min (+)	−	✓	−	−

Source: Data from the PSCS, Federal Bureau of Prisons, 2006–2010.
✓ = Supported; − = Unsupported; x = Significant in opposite direction as hypothesized.

Table 7.2   Results Summarized for Hypotheses 3 and 4

	2007	2008	2009	2010
		Hypothesis 3		
Individual Level				
Alienation (−)	✓	✓	✓	✓
Institutional Level				
Well-Super (+)	−	−	−	−
Treatment (+)	✓	−	−	−
Fear (−)	✓	−	−	−
Interactions				
Alienation•				
High Sec (−)	−	✓	✓	−
		Hypothesis 4		
Individual Level				
Alienation (+)	✓	✓	✓	✓
Institutional Level				
Well-Super (−)	−	−	−	−
Treatment (−)	−	−	−	−
Fear (+)	−	−	−	✓
Interactions				
Alienation•				
High Sec (+)	−	−	−	−
Alienation•				
Min Sec (−)	−	−	−	−

Source: Data from the PSCS, Federal Bureau of Prisons, 2006–2010.
✓ = Supported; − = Unsupported.

prisons does reach significance in two years). Notably, coercive power works counter to hypotheses and improves prisoner management across all four years of analysis. Table 7.2 highlights the significant and negative role that alienation plays on prisoner management and the significant and positive role that alienation plays on emotional hardening. These relationships gain significance across all four years. Importantly, institutional level factors fail to reach significance in the alienation models. However, the cross-level interaction of alienation in high-security prisons appears to be salient across two years (2008 and 2009).

The variance explained by the fully constructed models is also substantial. Not only do key predictors appear to have a robust relationship with the dependent variables (a relationship that holds across years) but they also appear to be vital to the explanation of the total variance. Fully constructed power adoption models explain between 35 and 40% of the variance of institutional commitment and between 25 and 27% of the variance of efficacy (Table 7.3). Alienation models explain between 24 and 27% of the variance of efficacy and between 20 and 23% of the variance of emotional hardening (Table 7.3).

Table 7.3   Variance Explained by Model

Year	2007	2008	2009	2010
Institutional commitment regressed on power adoptions				
Variance Explained R²Level 1	37.5%	40.8%	38.1%	35.4%
Variance Explained R²Level 2	48.9%	41.5%	26.7%	18.9%
Efficacy regressed on power adoptions				
Variance Explained R²Level 1	25.5%	27.5%	27.4%	26.2%
Variance Explained R²Level 2	53.1%	35.4%	64.9%	37.8%
Efficacy regressed on alienation				
Variance Explained R²Level 1	25.0%	27.9%	24.9%	27.5%
Variance Explained R²Level 2	69.8%	39.5%	69.3%	48.6%
Emotional hardening regressed on alienation				
Variance Explained R²Level 1	20.5%	23.9%	20.0%	21.0%
Variance Explained R²Level 2	41.8%	3.6%	71.9%	63.4%

Source: Data from the PSCS, Federal Bureau of Prisons, 2006–2010.

Since level-1 variables may explain level-2 variance, it is beneficial to compare institutional level variance explained in Model 1 with institutional variance explained in Model 2. This serves to isolate purely contextual effects (rather than compositional and contextual effects). Comparing Model 1 (without level-2 variables but with level-1 variables) and Model 2 (fully realized models) addresses these contextual effects. Although institutional-level factors are responsible for only a moderate amount of the total unexplained variance of the dependent variables, fully constructed models suggest that selected variables are fairly successful at explaining the remaining institutional level variation (which is often minimal). Between 18 and 48% of the level-2 variance of institutional commitment is explained by fully constructed models (Table 7.3). Between 35 and 64% of the level-2 variance of efficacy is explained in power models and between 39 and 69% is explained in alienation models (across four years, Table 7.3). Lastly, between 3 and 71% of level-2 variance of hardening is explained by the alienation models (Table 7.3). But due to the inconsistency in significance of key level-2 variables across years, these findings do not appear to aid in highlighting the importance of specific institutional level variables. It is worth noting, however, that unexplained variance—after the introduction of level-1 variables—is quite small at the institutional level. Analysis of compositional effects on variance indicates that institutional variance is reduced considerably by introduction of only level-1 variables to the models (not shown). With only level-1 predictors, unexplained level-2 variance is reduced by one-half for power predicting commitment, between 30 and 50% for power predicting efficacy, between 25 and 60% for alienation predicting efficacy, and between 20 and 76% for alienation predicting emotional hardening (not shown). The meaning of these specific findings are further discussed in Chapter 5.

LIMITATIONS

Perhaps the most significant limitation to this work is its inability to consistently predict outcomes at the institutional level. Institutional level hypotheses are largely unsupported by the results. Aggregations on the institutional level are assumed to capture relationships within the institutions. But these aggregations are simply institutional level averages and they may not capture actual internal dynamics. Aggregations of subjective reports may differ from an objective sense of that same reality. For example, research suggests that many prison workers have a favorable opinion of treatment but view their peers as having a strong custody approach (Cullen et al. 1989). Aggregations of individual perspectives will suggest the institution is largely treatment oriented when the objective and "false" sense of peer orientation may drive the institutional practice. Proxies for relationships with peers (custody-treatment orientation) and with prisoners (fear of prisoners) may not adequately address the overall relational aspects of the prison environment and for this reason they may not maintain significance across years. In addition, data for prisoner classification and infractions by prison (two level-2 variables of particular interest) were not available and are likely quite critical in the prediction of institutional commitment, efficacy, and hardening. Prisons with more aggressive populations probably increase the stress level of the prison workers. And it would be inappropriate to assume, for example, that all high-security prisons have identical populations. It is also important to note that the ICC across years for key outcome variables of hardening and efficacy is fairly small. Much of the variance of these two variables is explained at the individual level. In order to disentangle compositional and contextual effects, analyses evaluated the variance change between Model 1 and Model 2 (not shown). But further analysis suggests that a significant reduction in level-2 variation exists with the exclusive introduction of level-1 variables. This reduction is as much as 75% for emotional hardening in 2009 (not shown) and as little as 25% for efficacy in 2010 (not shown). Coupled with the fact that level-2 variables do not appear to be consistently related to outcomes across years, there are two potential conclusions to be drawn. The first, which appears highly likely, is that individual level factors are particularly important. The second claim is more speculative and suggests that institutional level factors may be masked by limitations of current identifiers. It is possible that even within security level the composition of prisoners varies (Camp et al. 2003). The effect of prisoners is largely evaluated on the institutional security level and this may hide differences within prisons of the same security level. Since key variables gain significance at the institutional level across all years but these variables fail to consistently reach significance (with the exception of fear in the prediction of commitment), this may be due to an inability to adequately account for prisoner composition. Camp et al. (2003) argue convincingly for use of custody scores rather than security levels for prisoner composition. Future studies should address the possibility of varying composition possibilities (beyond security level). But it cannot be overstated that the unexplained variance at the institutional level—after inclusion of individual level measures—is rather small.

Survey participation also fluctuates across years and certain years find participants less likely to answer questions presumably deemed to be sensitive or intrusive. It was necessary, therefore to construct a number of HLM files in order to maximize the number of observations per model. For example, the isolation measure in 2008 (not shown) has only 2373. This is a sizeable reduction from the number of observations in normlessness for the same year (not shown). Since four versions of the PSCS are administered it is only possible to construct measures of interest with half the total available number of observations. The questionnaire repeats each subject section in two of the four versions and repeats general information in all four of the versions. This may be less of an issue since analyses were conducted over four years.

It could be proposed that this study aims to understand objective power and management processes and yet employs survey data that is subjective interpretation. A prison workers' perception of effective prisoner management is not necessarily equivalent to his actual effectiveness in prisoner management and there is no way to confirm effectiveness through evaluations or through supervisor interview. It is conceded that behavioral measures would be preferable but these are not available.

Primary outcomes and predictor variables were constructed by alpha scores and by principal component factor analysis. Prior to these analyses, selection of components was based on compliance with theoretical structures. Final variable constructs do not necessarily represent the only possible configuration and may not—strictly speaking—fully represent the label they are given. In addition, alienation variables are highly correlated with one another and therefore single models were not run with full inclusion. This prevents a comparison across alienation variables in order to ascertain which measure is most salient a predictor of efficacy and of hardening.

FURTHER THEORETICAL ELABORATION

Results from this study engender a few complications that warrant further theoretical discussion (beyond the developed groundwork outlined in the previous chapter). At first glance, the results appear to illustrate an ironic contradiction in effective prison management. It is clear that federal correctional facilities promote constructive and formal power strategies. It is also clear that legitimate power adoptions correspond to increases in institutional commitment and increases in the perception of effective prisoner management. Belief in the just authority of the prison (of the BOP) improves the prison workers' perception of prisoner management (fostering progressive belief in prison work may be a critical next step for effective prison management). But it also appears that alienation strongly reduces effective prisoner management. If legitimate power interprets the institutional mission as a function of the keeper philosophy (and strict order maintenance), then alienated workers *theoretically* benefit prison management. Herein lies a dilemma in prison management. It is conceded that security is a reasonable primary focus for coercive institutions. But if a strict security focus promotes alienation, and alienated prison workers do not appear to benefit prisoners, then management may engender a strategy that has minimal net gain (particularly for the prisoner). In fact, results indicate that prison workers perceive their prison institutions to be legitimate and this sense of legitimacy improves perception in prisoner management.

But if legitimate power is defined solely by security measures, then this actually undermines effective prisoner management—hence, a potential net gain of zero. This illustrates the pertinence of the theoretical framework detailed in Chapter 6. Alienation is reduced by constructive power adoptions. It is likely, thereby, that a formal, transparent, and respectful authority can empower workers and engender a sense of collective importance—a sense of value in corrections. The major misconception in this discussion is not simply how alienation may be harmful or helpful but *where* it is valuable and *where* it is detrimental. The prison worker's dissociation from the prisoner may be beneficial (to a degree) and may improve his ability to complete his daily tasks with reduced physical and emotional burden. This same benefit, however, does not translate to the worker's relationship with his employer. Alienation from the employer does little but disrupt effective prisoner oversight—since the individual trumps the collective and the fear of personal accountability or failure is far more powerful than the shared communal success. I do not find this distinction troubling. Prisoners are not employees. Even though the worker may transfer his perceived foul treatment by his supervisor onto his charges it does not follow that the prisoner and the prison worker have a shared experience in terms of needs. The prisoner's situation would logically improve by a stronger collective correctional front that strictly reflects and endorses the administration's perspective. The proposal is not to construct factions of isolated prison workers. Instead, a strong, empathetic, and professional hierarchy that seeks to empower and ensures consistent and clear treatment protocols will benefit the prison worker and the prisoner. The prisoner may be able to derive meaning for his imprisonment and change his life. But demanding meaning in imprisonment beyond the dislike of such a state seems ridiculous. By definition, therefore, the prisoner and the prison worker operate in the same space and share similar experiences but are shaped by drastically different processes.

Fortunately, within the federal system, it appears that official channels of communication and constructive types of power affect prison workers. The analysis in this book suggests that there is little evidence that the prison worker opts out of official decrees (and instead relies on informal and destructive types of prisoner management). This is not to suggest that prison workers in federal prisons do not employ coercive power techniques. But rather institutions do not appear to informally endorse those techniques. The generation of factions is possible and even likely in most workplaces. But institutions do not appear to promote divergent normative conduct. Moreover, endorsed techniques—formal and constructive power strategies— improve the perception of prisoner management. Since it is unlikely that reductions in the alienation of the prison worker necessarily result in compromised security, it is counterproductive to pursue policies that effectively alienate workers. The aim is not to ensure prison workers reap benefit and meaning from prisoner oversight specifically, but rather that prison workers reap benefit from prison work specifically. These are different propositions in that the latter may be derived from the hierarchy, from peers, even from the general public. Therefore, the reduction in alienation may hail from superiors and from the administration through the generation of a unified, collaborative, and professional organization. Ultimately, the analysis and theoretical argument in this book promotes a perspective on coercive institutions that suggest malleability even within rigid environments. I do not believe that this necessarily lends itself to prisoner neglect. Prisoners are important. Humane and safe prisons for prisoners are a primary requisite of imprisonment. But meaning in prison work should not need to come from a population that is forcibly confined and has proven to be unable to abide by codified law. The right to imprison is of value to the prison worker in that it endorses the legitimacy of the institution itself. But the justification (or lack thereof) for specific sentences are a public issue and cannot overwhelm day-to-day supervision. If even one population of individuals is rationally and reasonably incarcerated then the right to imprison exists. The current use of prison may be unjust and unreasonable but that does not call for rejection of the entire practice.

Public support and recognition for prison work could conceivably undermine perceived meaninglessness in prison work. Public support may also empower prison workers to continue to adhere to the keeper philosophy even when aggravated by persistent manipulation, intimidation, or even verbal and physical assault. But prisons are largely isolated institutions, attracting only periodic public attention. The experience of imprisonment is not shared by the public. I argue, therefore, that value in prison work must come primarily from management. Prisons are largely out of sight of the public eye and do not generally interest the public beyond cost. I contend, therefore, that the prison administration must help to generate value for the worker. Indeed, pliability of management may be particularly useful in terms of alienation reduction. And this may be met in a variety of ways. Of course, dividing alienation measures into its components and running models separately admittedly precludes comparison across measures. But even though meaningful claims cannot be made regarding the most salient alienation predictor of emotional hardening and efficacy, reasonable conclusions can be drawn about the value of each independent alienation measure and its impact within the prison environment. This is invaluable insight for prison managers. All five individual measures—as well as the overall generated variable—are strong predictors of efficacy and of emotional hardening. And I propose that emotional hardening indicates early signs of dehumanization.

While dissociation, especially in moderation, may be beneficial, dehumanization is decidedly negative and deleterious to the prisoner and to the prison worker. Early stages of emotional hardening may be reversible and somewhat benign. The officer perceives that he is emotionally exhausted; he is growing irritable; he is beginning to treat prisoners like objects. It could be inferred that the authentically dehumanized worker objectively treats prisoners like objects and is not concerned or impacted by this cold treatment. The measure here, thereby, potentially captures early signs of severe dissociation. Of course, it is not a requirement that the progression follows necessarily and it is possible that acutely aware workers are more empathetic and reflective by nature and report greater concern over personal detachment and emotional exhaustion. Irrespective of this possibility, however, the outcome of hardening is not a productive or desirable disposition for prison workers. But it is possible that this worker is categorically distinct from the fully dissociated worker. Pursuing this logic, the analysis in this book specifically identifies key processes that aggravate effective treatment for the susceptible but not necessarily consumed prison worker. And even if they do not succumb to absolute dissociation, I propose that emotionally hardened prison workers are experiencing early signs of desensitization. Consistently robust (and significant) results suggest that reductions in individual level measures of alienation will counter this progression.

It is further possible that those prison workers who have already become fully "dehumanized" could benefit from reductions in alienation. I do not find convincing evidence that "dehumanization" is irreversible and, indeed, it seems contradictory to laud such a possibility when attempting to improve institutional management. Not only do I find it unlikely that "dehuman-ization" is a state without return but I also find the supposition unhelpful theoretically and practically in shaping prison management and improving prison oversight for the prison worker and for the prisoner. Regardless of the degree of dissociation, I contend that management process may diminish (and therefore prove malleable) dehumanization and objectification of pris-oners. Of course, solutions to alienation are somewhat vague. Especially in reference to a specific cure. A single solution to a complex problem seems unlikely and counter to the essential propositions of the alienation discussion. Constructing meaning and collective pride is, ironically, an individual pursuit and demands attention to the unique qualities of the specific prison worker population. Therefore, specific solutions may be vague but specific strategies are less obscure. Indeed, individual measures of alienation are far less opaque than the general conceptualization. Progressive and clever prison manag-ers would be able to directly reduce each specific alienation measure even within the confines of a strict security philosophy. Improving the independent alienation measures not only improves the perception of effective prisoner management but also reduces emotional hardening (and the potential physi-cal and mental complications that arise from it). It is plausible, moreover, that simple attempts to empower, to communicate, to coalesce will result in an improved worker perception. Objective realities may not dramatically improve but subjective interpretation of these realities may—and this latter transformation may have a substantial impact on the well-being and effec-tiveness of the prison worker.

Beyond speculative outcomes of the prison management strategies pro-posed by DiIulio (1987), ethnographic (Tracy 2008; Tracy and Scott 2006) and empirical work (Poole and Regoli 1981) suggest that alienation is preva-lent within prison worker populations and potentially a cause for concern. Results from this study suggest that alienation has specific negative outcomes on prison management. Combined with the above conclusions about power adoptions in coercive institutions, I have also proposed the advancement of a theoretical framework that specifically focuses on the nature of confinement. Unlike criminological theories that propose reasons for crime commission, this criminal justice theory proposes an inevitable impact of modern coercive institutions on prison workers and on prisoners. But, unsurprisingly, this framework is shaped by power strategies. Indeed, prisons are really about power and power therefore shapes outcomes within the institutional settings. Carefully selecting constructive power adoptions may be paramount. But prisons are complex and nuanced environments. And prison workers are human actors. I propose that it is preferable to consider alienation *and* power in tandem. Fair treatment, empowerment, and collective responsibility are critical for prison workers in prison.

NEXT STEPS

Future research should replicate these findings in state institutions. Future research should also attempt to address causality (this was not possible due to the cross-sectional nature of the data). But in particular, research should further evaluate: (1) the generation, perception, and employment of power within facilities and (2) the impact of alienation and power adoptions on efficacy and emotional hardening. Further attempts should also be made to understand what specifically reduces prison workers' perception of innovations within facilities. This is not a question of belief in programming or in treatment per se, but rather an inquiry into whether workers will accept novel approaches to actual prisoner management. Future research should also assess differences in prisoner populations across similar security levels and ascertain those effects on prison worker commitment and efficacy. Research in corrections should also target differences across prisons and begin to address uniformity. All prison institutions are not homogenous. Research should begin to assess divergence, specifically evaluating whether prisons vary in recidivism rates of released offenders.

CLOSING CONSIDERATIONS

Close to 1% of the US adult population is incarcerated (Pew Center on the States 2009). Human actors choose to watch this sizeable incapacitated population. And yet it is difficult to understand what drives the research regarding the watchers of this population. Great intrigue surrounds reentry but little focus targets prison workers. I believe that prison workers are integral and vital players in the justice system, executing a difficult and often-overlooked or ridiculed job. Past decades saw an explosion of research that was theoretically promising and methodologically (at the time) rigorous. The 1980s and early 1990s produced important studies on alienation and power. But this line of questioning appears to have largely dissolved and been replaced with less critical research questions. The prison literature could use an injection of theory and active narrative—beyond implicit and perhaps unfounded assumptions. The overall value of this pursuit is substantive. Recent years seem to reflect an obsession with the collection of outcomes (such as stress, burnout, role conflict) rather than an obsession with critical questions and organizing principles.

An organizing principle is needed. This principle should combine the limitations of prison environments—or the inevitable nature of prison—with a clear discussion of what we want prisons to accomplish and what we expect and demand from prison administrators and from prison workers. In part,

I have advanced security-first models as essential but incomplete. The prison institution is necessarily rigid but prison management is somewhat malleable. Here, prison worker alienation becomes theoretically important because it might reduce (or increase) formal control; prison worker dehumanization becomes theoretically important because it might reduce the officer's ability to garner information from prisoners and prevent potentially violent riots. In this way, deleterious effects of prison on prison management are placed into a flexible framework where improvement and change are possible.

Prisons are central to justice in the United States and there is little indication that they are an undesired institution. But the conversation must return to purpose: what do we want from prisons and what do we require, as citizens, from them? I have reasoned for elevated rationality. This requires specific philosophical reasons for individual imprisonment and collective justification for prison itself. Each prisoner should know the specific rationale for her individual imprisonment. I do not discount the value of retribution or incapacitation. I do ask that the state acknowledge the specific purpose of a prison sentence. This requires intentional prisons, and intentional prisons recognize the integral role of prison workers in generating safe and secure prisons and in shaping prison morality and culture.

References

Aiken, Michael, and Jerald Hage. 1966. "Organizational alienation: A comparative analysis." *American Sociological Review* 4:497–507.

Akers, Ronald. 1977. *Deviant Behavior: A Social Learning Approach* (2nd ed.). Belmont, CA: Wadsworth Publishing.

Anderson, Elijah. 1999. *Code of the Street: Decency, Violence and Moral Life of the Inner City*. New York: W.W. Norton.

Andrews, Donald A., and James Bonta, 2006. *The Psychology of Criminal Conduct* (4th ed.). Cincinnati, OH: Anderson.

Barry, John Vincent. 1956. "Pioneers in Criminology. XII. Alexander Maconochie (1787–1860)." *Journal of Criminal Law, Criminology, and Police Science* 47:145–161.

Beccaria, Cesare. 1995 [1764]. *On Crimes and Punishments and Other Writings*. New York: Cambridge University Press.

Bennett, James V. 1970. *I Chose Prison*. New York: Alfred A. Knopf.

Bierie, David M. 2012. "The impact of prison conditions on staff well-being." *International Journal of Offender Therapy and Comparative Criminology* 56:81–95.

Bierie, David M. 2013. "Procedural justice and prison violence: Examining complaints among federal inmates (2000–2007)." *Psychology, Public Policy, and Law* 19:15–29.

Blumstein, A., and A.J. Beck. 1999. "Population growth in U.S. prisons, 1980–1996." In *Prisons*, edited by Michael Tonry and Joan Petersilia, 1–16. Chicago: University of Chicago Press.

Blumstein, Alfred, and Jacqueline Cohen. 1973. "A theory of the stability of punishment." *Journal of Criminal Law and Criminology* 64:198–207.

Blumstein, Alfred, and Joel Wallman, eds. 2006. *The Crime Drop in America*. New York: Cambridge University Press.

Bottoms, Anthony, and Justice Tankebe. 2012. "Beyond procedural justice: A dialogic approach to legitimacy in criminal justice." *Journal of Criminal Law and Criminology* 102:119–170.

Britton, Dana M. 1997. "Perceptions of the work environment among correctional officers: Do race and sex matter?" *Criminology* 35:85–106.

Camerino, Donatella, Madeleine Estryn-Behar, Paul Maurice Conway, Beatrice Isabella Johanna Maria van Der Heijden, and Hans-Martin Hasselhorn. 2008. "Work-related factors and violence among nursing staff in the European NEXT study: A longitudinal cohort study." *International Journal of Nursing Studies* 45:35–50.

Camp, Scott D. 1994. "Assessing the effects of organizational commitment and job satisfaction on turnover: An event history approach." *The Prison Journal* 74:279–305.

Camp, Scott D., Gerald G. Gaes, Neal P. Langan, and William G. Saylor. 2003. "The influence of prisons on inmate misconduct: A multilevel investigation." *Justice Quarterly* 20:501–533.

Camp, Scott D., William G. Saylor, and Miles D. Harer. 1997. "Aggregating individual-level evaluations of the organizational social climate: A multilevel investigation of the work environment at the Federal Bureau of Prisons." *Justice Quarterly* 14:739–761.

Caplow, Theodore, and Jonathan Simon. 1999. "Understanding prison policy and population trends." *Crime and Justice* 26:63–120.

Carnahan, Thomas, and Sam McFarland. 2007. "Revisiting the Stanford Prison Experiment: Could participant self-selection have led to the cruelty?" *Personality and Social Psychology Bulletin* 33:603–614.

Carroll, Leo. 1998. *Lawful Order: A Case Study of Correctional Crisis and Reform.* New York: Garland Publishing.

Carson, E. Ann, and Daniela Golinelli. 2013. *Prisoners in 2012: Trends in Admissions and Releases, 1991–2012.* Bureau of Justice Statistics NCJ 243920. Washington, DC: US Department of Justice.

Carson, E. Ann, and William J. Sabol. 2012. *Prisoners in 2011.* Bureau of Justice Statistics NCJ 239808. Washington, DC: US Department of Justice.

Cloward, Richard. 1968. "Social control in the prison." In *Prison within Society: A Reader in Penology,* edited by Lawrence Hazelrigg, 78–112. Garden City, NY: Doubleday.

Cullen, Francis T., and Paul Gendreau. 2000. "Assessing correctional rehabilitation: Policy, practice, and prospects." In J. Horney (Ed.), *Criminal justice 2000: Vol. 3. Policies, processes, and Decisions of the Criminal Justice System* (pp. 109–175). Washington, DC: National Institute of Justice, U.S. Department of Justice.

Cullen, Francis T., Edward J. Latessa, Velmer S. Burton, Jr., and Lucien X. Lombardo. 1993. "The correctional orientation of prison wardens: Is the rehabilitative ideal supported?" *Criminology* 31:69–92.

Cullen, Frank T., Faith E. Lutze, Bruce G. Link, and Nancy Travis Wolfe. 1989. "The correctional orientation of prison guards: Do officers support rehabilitation?" *Federal Probation* 53:33–42.

Davis, Angela. 2003. *Are Prisons Obsolete?* New York: Seven Stories Press.

Dean, Dwight G. 1961. "Alienation: Its meaning and measurement." *American Sociological Review* 26:753–758.

Decker, Scott H., Cassia Spohn, Natalie R. Ortiz, and Eric Hedberg. 2014. *Criminal Stigma, Race, Gender and Employment: An Expanded Assessment of the Consequences of Imprisonment for Employment.* Final report to the National Institute of Justice. Retrieved from https://www.ncjrs.gov/pdffiles1/nij/grants/244756

DiIulio, John. 1987. *Governing Prisons: A Comparative Study of Correctional Management.* New York: Free Press.

DiIulio, John J., Jr. 1991a. *No Escape: The Future of American Corrections.* New York: Basic Books.

DiIulio, John J., Jr. 1991b. "Understanding prisons: The new old penology." *Law and Social Inquiry* 16:65–99.

DiIulio, John. 1995. "The coming of the super-predators." *Weekly Standard* 1:23–29.

Dowden, C., and C. Tellier. 2004. "Predicting work-related stress in correctional officers: A meta-analysis." *Journal of Criminal Justice* 32:31–47.

Durkheim, Emile. 1951 [1897]. *Suicide: A Study in Sociology.* New York: Free Press.

Durose, Matthew R., Alexia D. Cooper, and Howard N. Snyder. 2014. *Recidivism of Prisoners Released in 30 States in 2005: Patterns from 2005 to 2010.* Bureau of Justice Statistics NCJ 244205. Washington, DC: US Department of Justice.

Faris, Robert E., and Henry W. Dunham. 1939. *Mental Disorders in Urban Areas: An Ecological Study of Schizophrenia and Other Psychoses.* Chicago: University of Chicago Press.

Farkas, Mary Ann. 1999. "Correctional officer attitudes toward inmates and working with inmates in a 'get tough' era." *Journal of Criminal Justice* 27:495–506.

Feeley, Malcolm, and Jonathan Simon. 1992. "The New Penology: Notes on the emerging strategy of corrections and its implications." *Criminology* 30:449–476.

Fellner, Jamie. 2010. "Ensuring progress: Accountability standards recommended by the National Prison Rape Elimination Commission." *Pace Law Review* 30:1625–1645.

Foucault, Michel. 1977. *Discipline and Punish: The Birth of the Prison.* New York: Random House.

Frankel, M.E. 1972. "Lawlessness in sentencing." *University of Cincinnati Law Review* 41:1–54.

Freud, Sigmund. 1961 [1930]. *Civilization and Its Discontents.* New York: W.W. Norton.

Friedman, Lawrence. 1993. *Crime and Punishment in American History.* New York: Basic Books.

Gest, Ted. 2014, May 22. "U.S. conservatives: We're leading criminal justice reform." *The Crime Report.* Retrieved from http://www.thecrimereport.org

Glaze, Lauren E., and Erin J. Herberman. 2013. *Correctional Populations in the United States, 2012.* Bureau of Justice Statistics NCJ 243936. Washington, DC: US Department of Justice.

Goffman, Erving. 1961. *Asylums: Essays on the Social Situation of Mental Patients and Other Inmates.* Garden City, NY: Anchor Books.

Harcourt, Bernard E. 2011. "Reducing mass incarceration: Lessons from the deinstitutionalization of mental hospitals in the 1960s." *Ohio State Journal of Criminal Law* 9:53–88.

Hepburn, John R. 1985. "The exercise of power in coercive organizations: A study of prison guards." *Criminology* 23:145–164.

Hepburn, John R., and Celesta Albonetti. 1980. "Role conflict in correctional institutions." *Criminology* 17:445–459.

Hepburn, John R., and P. Knepper. 1993. "Correctional officers as human service workers: The effect of job satisfaction." *Justice Quarterly* 10:315–335.

Jackson, D., and J. Clare, and J. Mannix. 2002. "Who would want to be a nurse? Violence in the workplace—a factor in recruitment and retention." *Journal of Nursing Management* 10:13–20.

Jackson, Jerome, and Sue Ammen. 1996. "Race and correctional officers' punitive attitudes toward treatment programs for inmates." *Journal of Criminal Justice* 24:153–166.

Jurik, Nancy C. 1985. "Individual and organizational determinants of correctional officer attitudes toward inmates." *Criminology* 23:523–540.

Jurik, Nancy C., and Michael C. Musheno. 1986. "The internal crisis of corrections: Professionalization and the work environment." *Justice Quarterly* 3:457–480.

Kaplan, Thomas. 2014, April 3. "Cuomo drops plan to use state money to pay for college classes for inmates." *New York Times*, p. A23.

Kraska, Peter B. 2006. "Criminal justice theory: Toward legitimacy and an infrastructure." *Justice Quarterly* 23(2):167–185.

Lambert, Eric G., Calvin Edwards, Scott D. Camp, and William G. Saylor. 2005. "Here today, gone tomorrow, back again the next day: Antecedents of correctional absenteeism." *Journal of Criminal Justice* 33:165–175.

Lambert, Eric G., Nancy L. Hogan, and Shannon M. Barton. 2002. "Satisfied correctional staff: A review of the literature on the correlates of correctional staff job satisfaction." *Criminal Justice and Behavior* 29:115–143.

Langan, Patrick A., and David J. Levin. 2002. *Recidivism of Prisoners Released in 1994.* Bureau of Justice Statistics Special Report NCJ 193427. Washington, DC: US Department of Justice.

Liebling, Alison. 2004. *Prisons and Their Moral Performance: A Study of Values, Quality, and Prison Life.* New York: Oxford University Press.

Liebling, Alison. 2011. "Distinctions and distinctiveness in the work of prison officers: Legitimacy and authority revisited." *European Journal of Criminology* 8:484–499.

Liebling, Alison, David Price, and Guy Shefer. 2011. *The Prison Officer.* New York: Routledge.

Lombardo, Lucien X. 1989. *Guards Imprisoned.* New York: Elsevier.

MacKenzie, Doris Layton. 2006. *What Works in Corrections: Reducing the Criminal Activities of Offenders and Delinquents.* New York: Cambridge University Press.

MacKenzie, Doris Layton, David Bierie, and Ojmarrh Mitchell. 2007. "An experimental study of a therapeutic boot camp: Impact on impulses, attitudes and recidivism." *Journal of Experimental Criminology* 3:221–246.

Marquart, James W. 1986. "Prison guards and the use of physical coercion as a mechanism of prisoner control." *Criminology* 24:347–366.

Marquart, James W., and Julian B. Roebuck. 1985. "Prison guards and 'snitches.'" *The British Journal of Criminology* 25:217–233.

Martinson, Robert. 1974. "What works? Questions and answers about prison reform." *Public Interest* 35:22–54.

Maslach, Christina. 1978. "The client role in staff burn-out." *Journal of Social Issues* 34:111–124.

Maslach, Christina, and Susan E. Jackson. 1981. "The measurement of experienced burnout." *Journal of Organizational Behavior* 2:99–113.

Maslach, Christina, Wilmar B. Schaufeli, and Michael P. Leiter. 2001. "Job burnout." *Annual Review of Psychology* 52:397–422.

Merton, Robert K. 1938. "Social structure and anomie." *American Sociological Review* 3:672–688.

Minton, Todd. 2012. *Jail Inmates at Midyear 2011—Statistical Tables.* Bureau of Justice Statistics NCJ 237961. Washington, DC: US Department of Justice.

Mitchell, Ojmarrh, Doris L. MacKenzie, Gaylene J. Styve, and Angela R. Gover. 2000. "The impact of individual, organizational, and environmental attributes on voluntary turnover among juvenile correctional staff members." *Justice Quarterly* 17:333–357.

Morris, Norval, and David Rothman, eds. 1995. *The Oxford History of the Prison: The Practice of Punishment in Western Society.* New York: Oxford University Press.

Morris, Norval, and Michael Tonry. 1990. *Between Prison and Probation: Intermediate Punishments in a Rational Sentencing System.* New York: Oxford University Press.

Nagin, Daniel, Frank T. Cullen, and C.L. Johnson. 2009. "Imprisonment and reoffending." *Crime and Justice: A Review of Research* 38:115–200.

National Research Council. 2014. *The Growth of Incarceration in the United States: Exploring Causes and Consequences. Committee on Causes and Consequences of High Rates of Incarceration,* edited by Jeremy Travis, Bruce Western, and S. Redburn. Committee on Law and Justice, Division of Behavioral and Social Sciences and Education. Washington, DC: National Academies Press.

Paboojian, Aliene, and Raymond H.C. Teske, Jr. 1997. "Pre-service correctional officers: What do they think about treatment?" *Journal of Criminal Justice* 25:425–433.

Page, Joshua. 2011. *The Toughest Beat: Politics, Punishment, and the Prison Officers Union in California.* New York: Oxford University Press.

Paternoster, Raymond. 2010. "How much do we really know about criminal deterrence?" *Journal of Criminal Law and Criminology* 100:765–824.

Paternoster, Raymond, Robert Brame, Ronet Bachman, and Lawrence W. Sherman. 1997. "Do fair procedures matter? The effect of procedural justice on spouse assault." *Law and Society Review* 31:163–204.

Petersilia, Joan. 2003. *When Prisoners Come Home: Parole and Prisoner Re-Entry.* Oxford, UK: Oxford University Press.

Pettit, Becky. 2012. *Invisible Men: Mass Incarceration and the Myth of Black Progress.* New York: Russell Sage Foundation.

Pettit, Becky, and Bruce Western. 2004. "Mass imprisonment and the life course: Race and class inequality in U.S. incarceration." *American Sociological Review* 69:151–169.

Pew Center on the States. 2008. *One in 100: Behind Bars in America 2008*. Pew Charitable Trusts. Retrieved from http://www.pewtrusts.org/~/media/Imported-and-Legacy/uploadedfiles/wwwpewtrustsorg/reports/sentencing_and_corrections/onein100pdf.pdf

Pew Center on the States. 2009. *One in 31: The Long Reach of American Corrections*. Pew Charitable Trusts. Retrieved from http://www.pewtrusts.org/~/media/Assets/2009/03/02/PSPP_1in31_report_FINAL_WEB_32609.pdf

Pew Center on the States. 2011. *State of Recidivism: The Revolving Door of America's Prisons*. Pew Charitable Trusts. Retrieved from http://www.pewstates.og/uploadedFiles/PCS_Assets/2011/Pew_State_of_Recidivism.pdf

Pew Charitable Trusts. 2013. U.S. Prison Count Continues to Drop [Press Release]. Retrieved from http://www.pewstates.org/news-room/press-releases/us-prison-count-continues-to-drop-85899457496

Philliber, Susan. 1987. "Thy brother's keeper: A review of the literature on correctional officers." *Justice Quarterly* 4:9–37.

Piquero, Alex R., and Greg Pogarsky. 2002. "Beyond Stafford and Warr's reconceptualization of deterrence: Personal and vicarious experiences, impulsivity, and offending behavior." *Journal of Research in Crime and Delinquency* 39:153–186.

Pogarsky, Greg. 2002. "Identifying 'deterrable' offenders." *Justice Quarterly* 19:431–452.

Pogarsky, Greg, and Alex R. Piquero. 2003. "Can punishment encourage offending? Investigating the 'resetting' effect." *Journal of Research in Crime and Delinquency* 40:95–120.

Poole, Eric D., and Robert M. Regoli. 1980a. "Examining the impact of professionalism on cynicism, role conflict, and work alienation among prison guards." *Criminal Justice Review* 5:57–65.

Poole, Eric D., and Robert M. Regoli. 1980b. "Role stress, custody orientation, and disciplinary actions: A study of prison guards." *Criminology* 18:215–226.

Poole, Eric D., and Robert M. Regoli. 1981. "Alienation in prison: An examination of the work relations of prison guards." *Criminology* 19:251–270.

Raudenbush, Stephen W., and Anthony S. Bryk. 2002. *Hierarchical Linear Models: Applications and Data Analysis Methods* (2nd ed.). Thousand Oaks, CA: Sage.

Regoli, Robert M., Eric D. Poole, and Jeffery L. Schrink. 1979. "Occupational socialization and career development: A look at cynicism among correctional institution workers." *Human Organization* 38:183–187.

Roberts, John W. 1997. "The Federal Bureau of Prisons: Its mission, Its history, and its partnership with probation and pretrial services." *Federal Probation* 61:53–57.

Rogers, Everett M. 2003. *Diffusion of Innovations* (5th ed.). New York: Free Press.

Rothman, David J. 1990. *The Discovery of the Asylum: Social Order and Disorder in the New Republic* (revised edition). New Brunswick, NJ: Aldine Transaction.

Rothman, David J. 1995. "Perfecting the Prison." In *The Oxford History of the Prison*, edited by Norval Morris and David J. Rothman, 100–116, New York: Oxford University Press.

Rousseau, Jean-Jacques. 2005 [1762]. *The Social Contract.* New York: Barnes & Noble.

Ruth, H.S., and K.R. Reitz. 2003. *The Challenge of Crime: Rethinking Our Response.* Cambridge, MA: Harvard University Press.

Sampson, Robert J., and Charles Loeffler. 2010. "Punishment's place: The local concentration of mass incarceration." *Daedalus* 139:20–31.

Samuels, Charles E. 2014. "Memorandum for all Bureau inmates." *Inmate Admission and Orientation Handbook.* Federal Bureau of Prisons. Washington, DC: US Department of Justice.

Savelsberg, Joachim. 1992. "Law that does not fit society: Sentencing guidelines as a neoclassical reaction to the dilemmas of substantivized law." *American Journal of Sociology* 97:1346–81.

Saylor, William G. 1984. *Surveying Prison Environments.* Washington, DC: Federal Bureau of Prisons.

Saylor, William G. 2006. Comments on the design of the Prison Social Climate Survey. *Unpublished manuscript.*

Saylor, William G., Evan B. Gilman, and Scott D. Camp. 1996. "Prison Social Climate Survey: Reliability and validity analyses of the work environment constructs." Office of Research and Evaluation. Washington, DC: Federal Bureau of Prisons.

Schaufeli, Wilmar, and Maria C.W. Peeters. 2000. "Job stress and burnout among correctional officers: A literature review." *International Journal of Stress Management* 7:19–48.

Schwirtz, Michael. 2014, May 22. "Inmate attacks on civilian staff climb at Rikers." *New York Times*, p. A1.

Seeman, Melvin. 1959. "On the meaning of alienation." *American Sociological Review* 24:782–791.

Shaw, Clifford, and Henry McKay. 1942. *Delinquency and Urban Areas.* Chicago: University of Chicago Press.

Sherman, Lawrence W. 1993. "Defiance, deterrence, and irrelevance: A theory of the criminal sanction." *Journal of Research in Crime and Delinquency* 30:445–473.

Sherman, Lawrence W., and Heather Strang. 2007. *Restorative Justice: The Evidence.* London: Smith Institute.

Sparks, J. Richard, and Anthony Bottoms. 1995. "Legitimacy and Order in Prisons." *British Journal of Sociology* 46:45–62.

Stephan, James J. 2008. *Census of State and Federal Correctional Facilities, 2005.* Bureau of Justice Statistics NCJ 222182. Washington, DC: US Department of Justice.

Strand, Paul. 2012, March 1. "Punishing taxpayers: US prison system run amok?" *CBN News.* Retrieved from http://www.cbn.com/cbnnews/us/2012/february/punishing-taxpayers-us-prison-system-run-amok/

Subramanian, Ram, and Alison Shames. 2013. *Sentencing and Prison Practices in Germany and the Netherlands: Implications for the United States*. New York: Vera Institute of Justice.

Sutherland, Edwin H., Donald R. Cressey, and David F. Luckenbill. 1992. *Principles of Criminology*. Lanham, MD: Rowman & Littlefield.

Sykes, Gresham M. 1956. "The corruption of authority and rehabilitation." *Social Forces* 34:257–262.

Sykes, Gresham M. 1958. *The Society of Captives: A Study of a Maximum Security Prison*. Princeton, NJ: Princeton University Press.

Toch, Hans. 1978. "Is a 'Correctional Officer,' by any other name, a 'Screw'?" *Criminal Justice Review* 3:19–35.

Toch, Hans, and John Klofas. 1982. "Alienation and desire for job enrichment among correctional officers." *Federal Probation* 46:35–47.

Tonry, Michael. 1996. *Sentencing Matters*. New York: Oxford University Press.

Tonry, Michael. 2009. "Explanations of American punishment policies: A national history." *Punishment and Society* 11:377–394.

Tracy, Sarah J. 2004. "The construction of correctional officers: Layers of emotionality behind bars." *Qualitative Inquiry* 10:509–533.

Tracy, Sarah J. 2008. "Power, paradox, social support, and prestige: A critical approach to addressing correctional officer burnout." In *The Emotional Organization: Passions and Power*, edited by Stephen Fineman. Malden, MA: Blackwell Publishing.

Tracy, Sarah J., and Clifton Scott. 2006. "Sexuality, masculinity, and taint management among firefighters and correctional officers." *Management Communication Quarterly* 20:6–38.

Tyler, Tom R. 1990. *Why People Obey the Law*. New Haven, CT: Yale University Press.

Tyler, Tom R. 2010. "Legitimacy in corrections: Policy implications." *Criminology and Public Policy* 9:127–134.

United States Department of Justice. Federal Bureau of Prisons. 2009. State of the Bureau 2009: The Bureau's Core Values. http://www.bop.gov/news/PDFs/sob09.pdf

United States Department of Justice. Federal Bureau of Prisons. 2010. State of the Bureau 2010. http://www.bop.gov/news/PDFs/sob10.pdf

United States Department of Justice. Federal Bureau of Prisons. 2011. About the Federal Bureau of Prisons (2011). http://www.bop.gov/news/PDFs/ipaabout.pdf

United States Department of Justice. Federal Bureau of Prisons. 2012/2013. Quick facts about the Bureau of Prisons. Retrieved from http://www.bop.gov/about/facts.jsp

United States Department of Justice. Federal Bureau of Prisons. 2014. Statistics. Retrieved from http://www.bop.gov/about/statistics/population_statistics.jsp

Useem, Bert, and Jack A. Goldstone. 2002. "Forging social order and its breakdown: Riot and reform in US prisons." *American Sociological Review* 67:499–525.

Useem, Bert, and Peter Kimball. 1989. *States of Siege: U.S. Prison Riots, 1971–1986*. New York: Oxford University Press.

Useem, Bert, and Anne M. Piehl. 2006. "Prison buildup and disorder." *Punishment and Society* 8:87–115.

Useem, Bert, and Anne M. Piehl. 2008. *Prison State: The Challenge of Mass Incarceration.* New York: Cambridge University Press.

Wacquant, Loïc. 2010. "Class, race and hyperincarceration in revanchist America." *Daedalus* 139:74–90.

Whitehead, John T., and Charles A. Lindquist. 1989. "Determinants of correctional officers' professional orientation." *Justice Quarterly* 6(1):69–87.

Wilson, James Q., and George L. Kelling. 1982. "Broken windows: The police and neighborhood safety." *Atlantic Monthly* 249:29–38.

Wooldredge, John, Timothy Griffin, and Travis Pratt. 2001. "Considering hierarchical models for research on inmate behaviors: Predicting misconduct with multilevel data." *Justice Quarterly* 18:203–231.

Young, Warren, and Mark Brown. 1993. "Cross-national comparisons of imprisonment." *Crime and Justice* 17:1–49.

Zimbardo, Philip G., Christina Maslach, and Craig Haney. 2000. "Reflections on the Stanford Prison Experiment: Genesis, transformations, consequences." In *Obedience to Authority: Current Perspectives on the Milgram Paradigm*, edited by Thomas Blass, 193–237. Mahwah, NJ: Lawrence Erlbaum Associates.

Index

About the Author

Stephen C. McGuinn is assistant professor of Criminal Justice at Quinnipiac University in Hamden, Connecticut. He received his AB in Philosophy from the University of Chicago in 2002, his MS in Social Work from Columbia University in 2006, and his PhD in Criminology and Criminal Justice from the University of Maryland in 2013. Prior to pursuing his doctorate, he worked as a mental health professional and Assistant Unit Chief on Rikers Island in New York City.

CPSIA information can be obtained at www.ICGtesting.com
Printed in the USA
BVOW07*0205181114

375526BV00002B/4/P